The Minoan World

The Minoan World

Arthur Cotterell

MICHAEL JOSEPH

For My Wife

First published 1979 by Michael Joseph Ltd,
44 Bedford Square, London WC1

Produced by Guild Publishing,
the Original Publications Department of
Book Club Associates

Set in Janson and printed in Great Britain by
Lowe & Brydone Limited, Thetford, Norfolk

ISBN 0 7181 1846 4

Frontispiece: 'La Parisienne', a detail from the
Camp Stool fresco found at Knossos

CONTENTS

Above: The Palace of Minos from the south showing
the horns of consecration and the South Propylon

1

Knossos:
the Palace of Minos

War. This is the idea that the capital of Crete, spread out below on the coastline, imprints on the mind of the visitor arriving by air. The massive Venetian fortifications starkly separate Iraklion from its suburbs and the countryside beyond. A passenger stepping onto the quayside could not but share this impression, since the outstanding feature of the old harbour remains the Venetian mole, which Morosini once so valiantly defended against the Turks and which in 1941 provided a temporary refuge for some thirty British soldiers as German paratroops overran the city. Candia, the former name for Iraklion, derives from El Khandak, the moat that the Saracens dug around their base in 825. Pirates rather than settlers, these Arabs from Spain held the island for 125 years, till the Greek emperors of Byzantium, no longer able to tolerate their disruption of trade and their assaults on other island possessions, made a determined effort to recover Crete. The Byzantine troops finally took Candia in 961: the city was ruthlessly sacked, a fate common in Cretan history.

Resistance to invaders – whether Roman, Saracen, Venetian, Turk, or German – has imbued the character of the present-day islanders with a sturdy independence as well as a strong pride. Early this century the latter expressed itself in the adoption of the name Iraklion, after the mythological hero Herakles, when the nearby excavations of Sir Arthur Evans were exciting world interest in Cretan antiquity. What was not clearly perceived at the time was that the splendid Minoan civilization he had uncovered antedated the ancient Greeks. It was in fact the mysterious prelude to Europe.

The superhuman labours of Herakles may have been a cycle of legend that collected around an historical lord of Tiryns, the heavily fortified city to the south of Mycenae in the Peloponnese. The archaeological discoveries of Heinrich Schliemann (1822–90) during the 1870s in this part of Greece had already startled everyone. Within the golden treasures of the shaft-graves at Mycenae he claimed to have looked upon Agamemnon. It seemed that Homer's epics of the Achaean Greeks and their princely halls were modelled on surviving memories of the Mycenaean Age, which ended about

Overleaf: Looking south from the Central Courtyard.
The stairway to the ceremonial upper halls is on the extreme right

The Venetian fortress
which dominates the
harbour of Iraklion

1150 BC. Having discovered the site of Troy as well as the seat of
Agamemnon, whose runaway sister-in-law Helen caused the
Trojan War, Schliemann widened his search for the other place-
names recorded in the epics. Knossos was one of these: it had sent a
contingent with the Achaean host. But Crete was still under the
repressive rule of the Turks and the pioneer archaeologist was
unable to acquire the site. Schliemann abandoned the project and
the opportunity to excavate Knossos fell to Arthur Evans (1851–
1941) in 1900, two years after Turkish rule ended. Had Schliemann
dug there he would have been very surprised by the contrast
between the buildings unearthed and those at Mycenae and
Tiryns. For Knossos is conspicuously devoid of fortifications.
Almost at once Evans realized he was dealing with something older
than the Mycenaean period. Here was the palace and capital of
Minos the Sea-King, who the Greeks dimly remembered had long
before the Trojan War ruled the Aegean with his navy. The
Minoan civilization was reborn.

The bus journey today from Iraklion to Knossos, some 5 kilometres southwards, underlines the difference between Mycenaean
and Minoan, between the Greeks and the pre-Greek inhabitants of
Crete. The comfortable municipal bus – showing on its front what
must be the most evocative destination in Europe: Knossos – passes
out of the Venetian defences at the Jesus Gate, picks its way

through quiet suburban streets, and then proceeds along a road flanked by stone walls and smallholdings. A gentle, winding road with noble cypresses and juicy cacti – a dish still favoured in some parts of Crete. A road not far from the sea, whose flat blue-greyish presence is always felt at Knossos itself. Beside the road a spray of poppies, red diadems like those worn by Minoan idols, recalls the visions of priest-kings, who alone consorted with the godhead. The bus often stops to drop local people laden with shopping; a mother and two daughters just manoeuvre a rush mat through the door. We move on, the seats now occupied only by visitors to the Palace of Minos. Ahead a road-sign announces Knossos, and a row of souvenir shops and tavernas face the leafy entrance to the site, which nestles unprotected by bastions, lion-gates, and encircling walls on the low hillsides of a quiet valley. The stream below the palace was never broad enough to carry boats.

Far distant are the battle-cries on the plain before Troy, the bitter feuds of Achaean warrior-chiefs, and the sea-borne raids of the Dorian Greeks, the ancestors of modern Cretans. Knossos is a replica of the Minoan cosmos: the complex structure and several storeys of the great palace – twice the size of the palaces at Phaestos and Mallia – reveals an unequalled delight in the joy of life. The builders of the first elaborate pile in Europe chose the simple companionship of low surrounding hills. Theirs was an unsullied world, open to earth, sea, and sky. So unlike the cities that followed this first European civilization was Knossos that its extensive ruins were misinterpreted by the Greeks as the labyrinth, the abode of the awful Minotaur in the Theseus legend. How strange that later inhabitants of the island overlooked the basic tenor of the Minoan world. Peace.

Nevertheless, Homer did preserve the tradition of sacral kingship. In the *Odyssey* we read of 'the mighty city of Knossos wherein Minos ruled in nine-year periods, he who held converse with mighty Zeus'. Plato understood Homer to mean that Minos was accustomed to come face to face with the god every nine years and that he derived his wise government and lawgiving from these meetings. In a later chapter we shall discuss the philosopher's interpretation of the poet's lines but there is little reason to doubt that the Minoan institution of kingship had a religious basis and religious functions. Missing from the *Odyssey* is mention of the place of the meetings: did they occur on a mountain, in a sacred cave, or in a special chamber within the palace itself? The fact that the Minoans built no great temples and carved no large statues of their deities indicates that worship took place in small sanctuaries. Whilst the cave at Skoteino, west of the palace, may have been the sacred cave of Knossos as Evans believed, the gods were also venerated under roofs constructed by human labour, their presence in the Palace of Minos being signalled by the double axe, the *labrys*, an emblem displayed as frequently and conspicuously in Minoan religion as the cross in Christianity. According to the description of the site in *The Palace of Minos at Knossos*, the 3,000-page work published by Evans between 1921 and 1935, one cannot avoid running into sacred emblems, small shrines, libation tables, and lustral chambers.

Access to the palace is gained via a modern entrance and a trellised path that winds through a grove of pine trees, in summer heat alive with complaining cicadas. The visitor today, like his ancient counterpart who would have probably approached by the road that comes over the viaduct from the south, must be struck by the beauty of the setting. Lying in front is the West Court, a broad area paved with irregular slabs of stone and crossed by several raised walks, one leading directly to the West Porch, the entry to the main reception rooms of the palace. Visible are many of the 'reconstitutions' undertaken by Evans during his long series of excavations, and these partial restorations of architectural features – though the butt of criticism, both informed and uninformed – blend perfectly with the landscape, reminding us that we behold an enormous house, the residence of gentle rulers; unarmed princes with flowing locks; handsome ladies, whether members of the aristocracy or attentive priestesses; and sacred dancers or acrobatic toreadors. Knossos exalts the feminine spirit, just as Minoan religion seems to have given a dominant role to goddesses.

A distinctive feature of the West Court, and doubtless the model for the smaller palaces at Phaestos and Mallia, are three large circular pits, *koulouras*. These appear to have been constructed as granaries rather than repositories for ritual offerings, because the eight smaller examples at Mallia retain their central pillars and suggest that each pit was domed. The prototype of the *koulouras*, a Greek word meaning round and hollow, may have been a store-

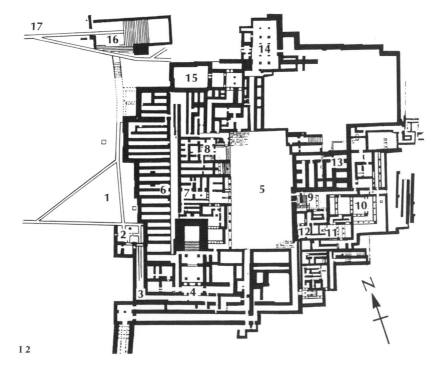

The Palace of Minos

1 West Court
2 West Porch
3 Corridor of the Procession
4 South Propylon
5 Central Court
6 West Magazine
7 Pillar Crypts
8 Throne Room
9 Grand Staircase
10 Hall of the Double Axes
11 Queen's Room
12 Court of Distaffs and toilet
13 Workshops
14 North Entrance
15 Large lustral basin
16 Theatral area
17 Royal Road or 'Sacred Way'

Above: A view across
the West Magazine to
the West Court

house underlying the south edge of the palace. This 'dungeon', as
Evans called it, was either a massive silo or a well; the dome-
shaped, underground chamber even possessed a staircase leading
down from the top. All Minoan palaces set aside considerable areas
on the ground floor for the storage of foodstuffs. At Knossos the
West Magazine, a long row of rooms opening off a north-south
corridor adjacent to the West Porch, contained the largest of all
facilities yet discovered. Originally it housed upward of 420 huge
clay jars, known as *pithoi*, as well as numerous cists sunk into the
ground. The storage capacity has been estimated at between
60,000 and 120,000 litres. Evans argued that the *pithoi* must have
contained oil, since no trace of grain was discovered in them, but
from the evidence of other sites it can be assumed that the Minoan
rulers stored oil, grain, and wine. There were also other magazines
in the palace.

The West Porch was the ceremonial entrance. The ancient
visitor would have observed the sparkling alabaster facade of the
main reception rooms high above him, before entering the guarded
portal and passing along the narrow Corridor of the Procession.

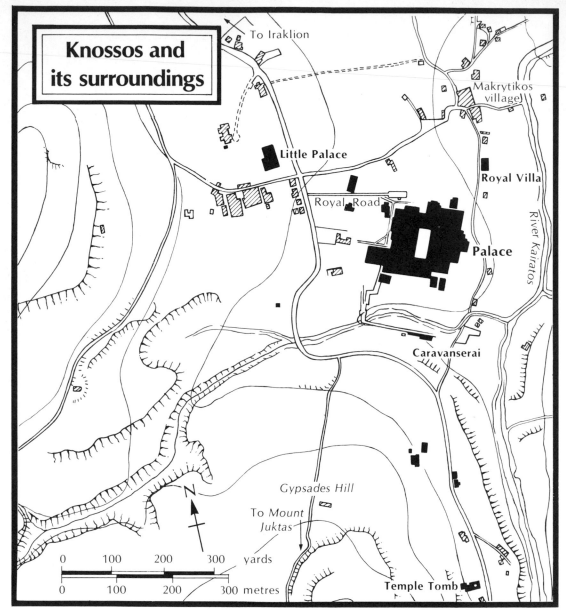

To Iraklion

Makrytikos village)

Little Palace

Royal Villa

Royal Road

Palace

River Kairatos

Caravanserai

N

Gypsades Hill

To Mount Juktas

| 0 | 100 | 200 | 300 | yards |
| 0 | 100 | 200 | 300 | metres |

Temple Tomb

The corridor heads south, turns east at the south-west corner of the palace, and through a formal inner entrance, the South Propylon, then offers the choice of ascending a fine staircase to the spacious upper halls or taking a few steps into the sunlit Central Court, an area measuring 50 by 25 metres and paved with rectangular slabs of limestone. In this indirect way of bringing an outsider into the inner parts of the palace we encounter a favourite conceit of Minoan architects: a circuitousness that must have fostered the notion of the labyrinth. Our present-day interpretation of a labyrinth as a place where one can easily lose one's way is at odds with the labyrinthine, confusing, yet testing journey of the soul that probably informed ancient Minoan belief. Another effect of the architectural design of Knossos is the focus on the Central Court and the ritual activities of the royal family in the main wings

Right: The South Propylon with reconstructions of the frescoes which lined it and the Corridor of the Processions

to the east and west. Once inside the palace the ancient visitor would have immediately appreciated the priestly role of the king. A clue exists in the traces of brightly painted figures on the wall of the Corridor of the Procession. Instead of the grandiose depictions of Egypt or Mesopotamia – lion hunts, battle scenes, booty, and wretched prisoners awaiting their dispatch – the fresco shows that a long procession was bringing presents to the king, or to a god. The atmosphere is easy and friendly, nothing like the overwhelming presence of the pharaohs, whose contemporary statues are measured in hundreds of tons. Neither the oppressive divinity of Egyptian monarchs nor the military prowess of Semitic rulers find a place in Minoan history. On the contrary, the Minoans seem to have delighted in a certain fullness of life. The processional fresco hints at a semi-rural tranquillity, a great palace and its surrounding city still intimate with natural things, a civilization not shut in by walls. The dividing line between human and divine, like that between town and country, is hard to distinguish too. We can never be quite sure in Minoan art that one figure is immortal and another is not.

Between the West Magazine and the Central Court are situated a number of cult rooms. Two of the inner rooms have stone pillars marked with the sacred symbol of the double axe, and on either side of the pillar nearest to the Central Court are shallow stone trays set in the floor. These receptacles for sacred offerings or libations reveal a cult of generation: ceremonies turning on the fruitfulness of the earth, as represented in the phallic associations of the post, and the cycle of birth, growth, decay, and death that encompasses plant, animal, and man. That first offerings of farm produce were made in the Pillar Crypts we can be fairly sure from their location next the West Magazine. The dark cave-like nature of the shrines adds another dimension, recalling sacred grottoes in which intoxicating drink was prepared from honey on festive occasions. At the New Year festival it was an ancient custom in the Aegean and Asia Minor to perform rites connected with fermentation, a natural process full of religious import for those concerned with death. Yet the subterranean world, the world of caves recreated in the pillar crypts, is extended and transformed elsewhere in the palace as the architecture of columns. At Knossos the column seems a potent symbol of life rising from the earth, the inviolable source of fertility and the shrouded abode of the dead.

In the many limestone caves that exist among the Cretan mountains we can discern the origins of the sacred post. Arcane and amazing to the modern archaeologist as well as the ancient worshipper, these innumerable recesses contain a forest of stalactites and stalagmites. Wedged in the crevices around such natural pillars were hundreds of votive bronzes including double axes. The cave at Amnisos, the harbour of Knossos, survived in the Greek period as a sanctuary of Eileithyia, goddess of childbirth. Its

Opposite: The sun sets behind the great horns of consecration at Knossos

16

Left top: The Grand Staircase in the Domestic Quarter

Left bottom: The Throne Room which was the first part of the palace to be excavated

Below: A reconstruction of the Throne Room. The shattered remains of the ritual jars in the foreground persuaded John Pendlebury that the last king had been surprised here by raiders

Right: The antechamber to the Throne Room. Evidence was found that a wooden throne had stood here

The 'holy of holies' inside the Cave of Eileithyia at Amnisos
showing the rectangular enclosure around a single stalagmite

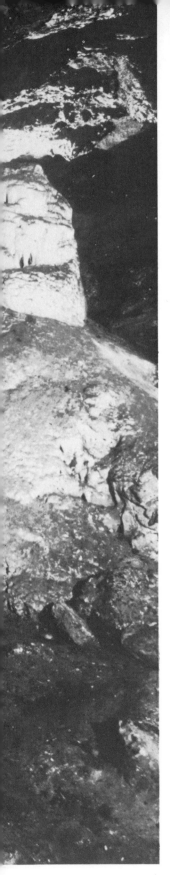

unusual double stalagmite may have inspired originally a concept of a dual goddess, as late Cretan art preserves this divinity. In Minoan times the twin goddesses presumably did more than over-look childbirth; as an aspect of the mother-goddess, they presided over everything in the life of women and their cave sanctuary was dedicated to natural abundance. Within the inner enclosure, a small rectangular space, there rises a solitary stalagmite, the up-thrusting presence of universal fertility. The phallus. Here it is, in uncarved rock, unmistakably present in the 'holy of holies' of a feminine shrine. Here is pillar worship in its most primitive and naturalistic form. Moreover, there are obvious connections be-tween the cult of the sacred pillar and that of the sacred tree. The Minoans surrounded the latter with walls and placed boughs on domestic altars. Although later scholars have questioned Evans' interpretation of the double axe as the aniconic image of the Minoan deity and argued that it was often used merely as a masons' mark, it would seem that he is correct in identifying the pillar crypts and finding tree and pillar worship inseparable.

North of the Pillar Crypts and the stairway leading from the Central Court to the ceremonial upper halls lies the famous Throne Room, where in 1900 Evans excavated an impressively carved stone chair standing upright against the north wall. This portion of the palace was the first to be dug and the discovery of the 'oldest throne in Europe' appeared to confirm all the legends of Minos, King of the Sea. Remains of large flat oil vases of gypsum and a large clay storage jar scattered over the floor gave the excavators the idea that the king and his councillors were performing some religious ceremony in this room when the palace was over-whelmed, perhaps to avert the disaster. Whatever the truth, the so-called Throne Room was the scene of ritual observances. The chamber is low-ceilinged and dark, its polished gypsum flagstones only faintly reflecting the brightness of the Central Court, while opposite the throne, a short flight of steps away, stands a lustral chamber used for ceremonial washing. As a priest-king, the ruler of Knossos might have been expected to perform here rites of purification connected with the adjacent Pillar Crypts. An alter-native view is that the throne belonged to a high priestess who, seated amid her companions, impersonated the Minoan mother-goddess, the Lady of the Labyrinth. In this case the king might have approached her as a divine consort, just as at the time of the New Year festival the ancient Sumerians celebrated a holy marriage between the king and the goddess of a city, represented by a priestess. The sacral coupling was believed to ensure prosperity, strength, and concord. A full discussion of such con-jectures will occur in our survey of religious beliefs; for the present it is enough to say that Evans' description of the Throne Room as place of ritual cannot be faulted because nothing has been found to suggest that it was a chamber for royal audiences. Not only were there more spacious rooms available for ceremonial purposes on

Looking across the
Central Courtyard from
the east showing the
State Apartments and
Evans' reconstruction of
part of the ceremonial
upper halls

the upper storeys, but even more the Hall of the Double Axes in the eastern wing was better suited for courtly affairs. Evans also thought that the Throne Room suite was inserted into the palace around 1400 BC, so that it could have been built under the direction of the Mycenaean Greek dynasty then in occupation of Knossos. The heraldic griffins, whose curved beaks are haughtily raised above feathered necks on each side of the throne, may be cousins of the beasts painted on the walls of the great hall of the Mycenaean palace at Pylos in the south-western Peloponnese, but the fresco along with the arrangement of the Throne Room is essentially Minoan.

When the rituals were finished, the king and his attendants must have stepped from the darkened rooms of the western wing and crossed the dazzling Central Court to the state appartments. Before looking at these well-preserved rooms in the east wing, termed the Domestic Quarter by Evans, a few words are needed on the role of central courtyards in Minoan palaces. Their importance can be seen at a glance from the plans of Knossos, Phaestos, and Mallia. Besides acting as the organizing nuclei of the layout, the open spaces around which the palace wings were built, they also formed the main thoroughfares of daily life. Porticoes and galleries along the sides ensured that they could accommodate spectators for public entertainments too. On their flagged expanses the Minoans would have watched boxing matches; dancing, perhaps still a sacred event; and the bull games depicted in various frescoes. At Phaestos there are traces of doors to protect all the openings on the Central Court, an architectural feature suggesting that bulls charged at will under the eyes of the people standing on the first floor. Although the bull may have been sacrificed at the end of the game, like the animal shown trussed before an altar on the famous sarcophagus from Hagia Triada, the performances were never bull fights, since the acrobatic toreadors carried no weapons. The most daring feat of these performers was to seize the horns of a charging bull and to turn a full somersault over the bull's back, thereby landing on the courtyard behind.

Thanks to the position of the private apartments of the royal family, safely cut into the hillside, and Evans' imaginative reconstruction of the different levels, the modern visitor is able to obtain a firm impression of the state rooms as they appeared in 1500 BC. It is a memorable experience to descend the Grand Staircase into the Domestic Quarter. 'The most daring exhibition of Minoan architecture' Evans called the stone stairway, once the means of reaching five storeys – one on the level of the Grand Court, two below, and two above. Constructed round a light-well, the Grand Staircase had two flights to each floor and rested upon large tapered columns of painted wood. At each storey the stairway let the ancient visitor into a hall and a suite of rooms that ended in a colonnaded verandah overlooking the gardens laid out along the

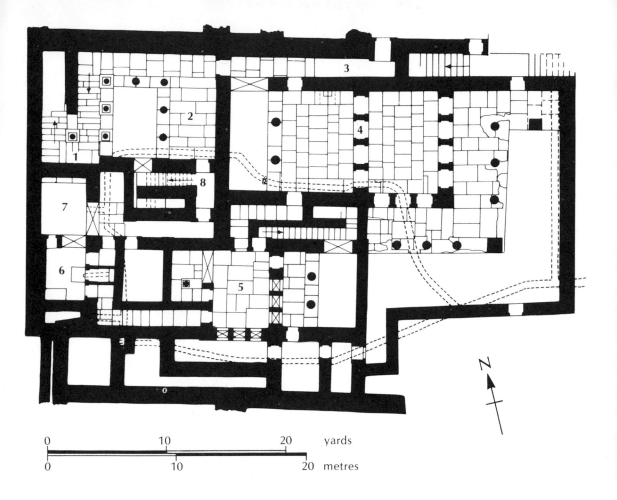

```
0          10          20    yards
|_____|_____|
0          10          20    metres
```

eastern side of the palace, next to the Kairatos riverlet. Even today at noon the visitor, cool and relaxed on the ancient stairs, can share the revery of Evans when one moonlit night he stood there and

the whole place seemed to awake awhile to life and movement. Such was the force of the illusion that the Priest-King with his plumed lily crown, great ladies, tightly girdled, flounced and corseted, long-stoled priests, and, after them, a retinue of elegant and sinewy youths – as if the Cup-bearer and his fellows had stepped down from the walls – passed and repassed on the flights below.

At the foot of the Grand Staircase is the Hall of the Colonnades, which is dominated by four huge columns of typical Minoan shape, shafts that taper downward instead of upward. From this impressive hall a corridor leads straight to the Hall of the Double Axes, so-called by Evans because of numerous double-axe symbols incised on the walls. The Hall of the Double Axes is a delightful double room measuring 8 by 12 metres overall. The inner half of the room, lighted at its west end via a light-well, is divided from the eastern half by a row of five rectangular pillars. The gaps between these pillars used to be closed in colder weather by sets of double wooden doors. The Hall of the Double Axes was

The Domestic Quarter

1 Grand Staircase
2 Hall of the Colonnades
3 Corridor to the North-east
4 Hall of the Double Axes
5 Queen's Room
6 Toilet
7 Court of the Distaffs
8 Service staircase

===== Drain

25

Above: The bottom of the Grand Staircase, showing the Hall of the Colonnades

Above right: The Queen's Room showing the famous dolphin fresco

probably the king's room: in it he may have slept, received important visitors, dispensed justice, performed other duties, and taken his pleasures. Outside an L-shaped verandah offered excellent views of the valley to the east and south. A private corridor from the inner room of the hall connects with the Queen's Room, noted for its beautiful frescoes of marine life and figures of dancing girls. The floor of the Queen's Room is flagged with gypsum and the ceiling painted with an intricate spiral pattern. A small garden may have been laid out in its light-well for the benefit of the court ladies.

Adjacent to the Queen's Room is the Bathroom, where the remains of a clay tub were found near the door. No bathtubs have been excavated in bathrooms – a circumstance that has encouraged argument over the use of these rooms: were they bathrooms dedicated to hygiene or lustral chambers associated with ritual purification? But as Minoan bathtubs were never fixed they could have been carried from the ruins and used for other purposes, like the burial of the dead. Large numbers of such clay tubs have been recovered from cemeteries. Whereas the lustral chamber next to the Throne Room in the western wing can be readily identified through its proximity to the Pillar Crypts, there seems little reason to suppose that the Bathroom in the Domestic Quarter had more than a sanitary purpose. The interest of the Minoans in physical comfort is likewise evident in the Toilet situated nearby in the Court of Distaffs. Toilets were a feature of Minoan architecture, though the water-borne arrangements here are the most elaborate known. Waste from the Toilet was flushed into the drainage system by means of water from a large pitcher and odours prevented from escaping upwards by a plug. During the winter months the rain that fell into the light-wells would have been sufficient to flush out all refuse.

North of the Domestic Quarter were rooms in which the palace craftsmen worked and stored their artefacts. These skilled work-

Left: The Queen's Bathroom

Right: A reconstruction of the Bathroom which appeared in *The Illustrated London News* in 1930

men – sculptors, potters, metallurgists, engravers, faience-makers, and lapidaries – met the needs of the palace, which was the chief centre of ancient technology. The priest-king supervised this production of luxury goods and his scribes kept records of what was held in the storerooms. No archive room, however, has been discovered at Knossos, clay tablets turning up at widely scattered points throughout the palace and its environs. Yet there is one instance of records being located along with the objects listed on them. In the northern wing Evans uncovered two piles of bronze arrow-heads, with remains of the wooden shafts, and a broken clay tablet listing two lots of arrows.

To the west of the North Entrance, which leads directly up a sloping passage to the Central Court, is a suite of rooms that may have been reserved for distinguished visitors. It was usual for Bronze Age palaces to have accommodation set aside for noble guests, whether senior members of the native aristocracy, foreign ambassadors, or friendly monarchs. The rulers of Egypt and

Mesopotamia had such facilities and Minoan Crete is unlikely to have been an exception. If this is the correct explanation of the north-west corner of Knossos, situated as it is so conveniently near a palace entrance, then the lustral chamber there is rather another bathroom. Like the one in the Domestic Quarter, it could have been furnished with a clay bathtub that servants would fill and empty by hand. Impressed by its size – the bathroom is larger and deeper than others on the site – Evans argued on the contrary that the function of this part of the palace was the purification of visitors before they gained admission. Today we cannot be sure, though the fragment of an alabaster jar inscribed with the name of the Hyksos king Khyan found in the area hints otherwise. This pharaoh reigned in the later seventeenth century BC and one of his officials might have travelled from Egypt to stay and wait upon the Minoan king.

The Theatral Area could have been used to receive important visitors. It is a flagged courtyard with terraces of low stone steps on the east and south sides: a platform at the junction of these terraces might have taken a wooden royal box. North of the West Court and hard by the guest suite at the North Entrance, the Theatral Area probably acted as the terminus for processions along the Royal Road, or Sacred Way, a raised stone walk leading from the Little Palace some 250 metres westwards. But the spectators crowding the shallow steps could have witnessed other spectacles because the construction is reminiscent of Homer's description of the 'dancing-place that in Knossos Daedalus wrought for Ariadne of the lovely tresses'. As the poet confers the ornamental epithet 'of the lovely tresses' more on goddesses than mortals the dancing-place might have been prepared for the goddess Ariadne rather

Above: The Theatral Area showing the platform which might have held a royal box on the right

Opposite: Looking back down the Royal Road towards the Theatral Area. This would have been lined with buildings

31

than Minos' daughter. While the Throne Room could have been occupied by the queen, or a high priestess, representing the Lady of the Labyrinth, the Theatral Area might have seen a dancing princess impersonate another aspect of the Minoan mother-goddess. Ariadne is the Cretan-Greek form for Arihagne, 'utterly pure', and in her purity she would have performed before the assembled nobility the intricate movements of her winding and unwinding dance. In Greek legend she became the king's daughter who gave to Theseus the famous thread by means of which he negotiated the labyrinth. Yet we can perhaps still glimpse in this later transformation the essence of the Minoan idea. Her dance celebrated the natural flowering of life; she was the vital element moving across the flagstones – the life within everything. Her dance also gave entry and exit to the mysterious labyrinth, the place of death; she was the guide of the spirit on the dangerous journey to the after-life.

The Royal Road stands now in a defile, but originally it was lined with substantial buildings, which seem to have been houses built over workrooms and stores. Behind these buildings, south of the roadway, is located the House of the Frescoes, where Evans recovered sheets of stucco painted with blue monkeys and birds. This find was all the more remarkable in such a small house because the fragile sheets were neatly stacked together. The wonderful naturalistic frescoes may have been awaiting their erection on a wall. They date from around 1500 BC.

In order to reach the Little Palace the modern visitor must leave the Royal Road and retrace his steps to the site entrance. A few paces up the road towards Iraklion, about 10 metres after the last taverna, there is on the left the gate leading to the Little Palace. This residence, measuring some 800 square metres, was built on an artificial terrace and faced the east. A large town house rather than a palace, it probably served members of the royal family as a place of retreat from state affairs. The Royal Villa on the opposite side of the valley no doubt met a similar need, though it has been suggested that this even smaller building had a religious or judicial function. The ground floor of the Little Palace comprises a double hall, a columned portico, inner rooms including a toilet, a bath-room and three pillar crypts, and stairways to the upper floor. In the final period of the building's existence the bathroom or lustral chamber was enclosed as a shrine. Rough stones were used to block the spaces between the original wooden pillars. Possibly this part of Knossos was occupied by squatters after the destruction of the main palace.

The artificial terrace on which the Royal Villa reposes was also joined by a short paved road to the northern wing of the palace. The most interesting features of the building are the recessed seat or throne, placed on a dais behind a balustrade in the double hall; the staircase which branches into two wings after the first landing, a unique arrangement in Minoan architecture; and the pillar crypt, the ceiling of which was supported by a system of huge split tree trunks resting on a central gypsum pillar and lodged in sockets in the masonry at the top of the walls. Evans estimated that the trunks were of a width of over 0.80 metres. In the floor of the crypt were sunk a channel and two cists, evidently intended to catch libations offered before the sacred pillar. Speculation as to the actual use of the Royal Villa continues among archaeologists, and the absence of storerooms of any kind on the ground floor encourages those who would argue that it was the scene of impressive ceremonies.

The burial of the royal dead one might suppose to have been a matter of prime concern at Knossos, considering the elaborate preparations made by Bronze Age rulers in Mesopotamia and Egypt. Strangely the only certain royal or princely tomb of the Minoan period is the Temple Tomb, discovered by Evans in 1931 nearly 600 metres south of the palace. Whilst it was plundered and reused after 1450 BC, the Germans caused the greatest damage during the Second World War. Originally the tomb had an upper storey and was entered from an enclosed open court from the east. An inner pillar crypt built against a low cliff led to a rock-cut burial chamber. The whole complex recalls the tomb of Minos in Sicily described by the historian Diodoros Siculus, who lived shortly before the time of Christ, as a concealed tomb below the earth and

A reconstruction of the Temple Tomb close to the Palace of Minos

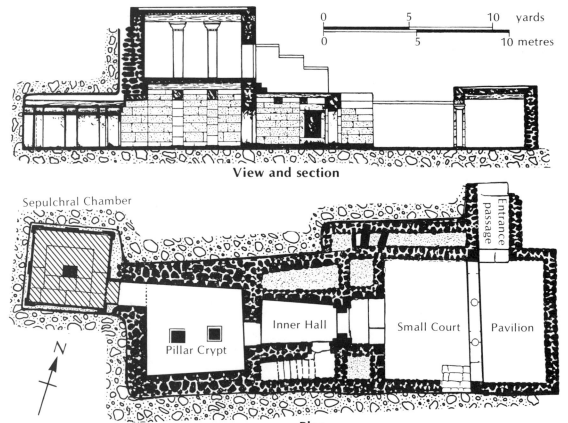

0   5   10   yards
0   5   10 metres

View and section

Sepulchral Chamber

Entrance passage

Inner Hall

Small Court

Pavilion

Pillar Crypt

N

Plan

Above: The south side of the palace showing how houses were built down the mound on which the palace stood. The so-called Priest's House is in the foreground

Right: The Palace of Minos seen from the east across the valley

a temple to the goddess Aphrodite above. Legend says that the king died at the city of Kamikos, on the western end of the island, when he sailed there to apprehend his fugitive engineer and architect, Daedalus. For the modern visitor to Knossos this tale provides a tantalizing glimpse, however distorted, of the former authority of this ancient palace city. From here sailed the fleets that sought to capture Daedalus and avenge Minos' death. No shore of the Mediterranean was safe for the renegade: no other monarch could be allowed to have the services of so brilliant a man.

Reflections such as these might well occupy the modern visitor walking back to the tavernas and bus-stop outside the palace entrance. Should he choose to pause at the Caravanserai before the bridge over the Kairatos, the impression of the past splendour of Knossos will be strengthened by the view of the palace, so well sketched and suggested by Evans' restoration. Here to the contemporary eye is disclosed the majestic outline of the palace of a great sea-king. No longer can the traveller wash his feet in the bath fed by spring water that bubbles up near the Caravanserai, which once served as a resting place and a shrine for the Minoans. Hospitality must be got in one of the tavernas, where a refreshing glass of wine is poured from a bottle labelled 'Minos'. Afterwards there is the bus trip to Iraklion and the twentieth century. In the capital, however, a rare treat still remains in store, the now famous Archaeological Museum. The range and variety of its collection of Minoan finds, not to mention their excellent display, fully justifies the decision taken by the Cretans immediately after the end of Turkish rule to restrict the export of antiquities from the island. Visits to the palace and the museum are the incredible starting points for a journey into the age of Europe's first civilization, which Evans named the Minoan world.

Opposite: The impressive Bull Portico at Knossos

2

Discovery: from Legend to Archaeological Site

In 1846 appeared a monumental study by George Grote entitled the *History of Greece*. Its author, an eminent historian, explained to the readers that his book commenced 'the real history of Greece with the first recorded Olympiad, or 776 BC. . . . For the truth is, that historical records, properly so called, do not begin until after this date'. All earlier events were merely the property 'of epic poetry and legend'. Of the Trojan War Grote concluded: 'Though literally believed, reverentially cherished, and numbered among the gigantic phenomena of the past, by the Grecian public, it is in the eyes of modern enquiry essentially a legend and nothing more . . . .We possess nothing but the ancient epic itself without any independent evidence.'

During the next sixty years the words of this scholar were to be made as archaic as the prehistory he dismissed. A profound alteration of outlook took place in the academic world: historians were compelled to reconsider the era before written records; their attitude to prehistoric incident was transformed by the archaeological discoveries of a number of enthusiasts. The two outstanding pioneers were Heinrich Schliemann and Sir Arthur Evans.

Heinrich Schliemann

Any account of the development of archaeology must include the modern investigator of Homer. As a child in Germany, Schliemann had been entranced by stories drawn from the epics, particularly the long struggle between the Trojans and the Greeks, but it was not until 1871 that he could test his conviction that somewhere under the ground were hidden the ruins of Troy. At the age of forty-nine he was then rich enough to retire from commerce and devote his life to 'digging for relics of the past'.

Although Schliemann was not the first investigator of the possible sites of Troy, his determination and wealth led to the crucial discovery. He employed a large force of workmen, 'three overseers and an engineer, to make maps and plans'. Even more

Opposite:
Sir Arthur Evans
(1851–1941)

39

A 19th-century engraving of the grave enclosure at Mycenae, with the Schliemanns in the centre viewing the site

important he, along with his new Greek wife, lived in a wooden house built on the mound at Hissarlik during the excavation. After three years of driving trenches into the mound and uncovering the remains of numerous cities, he announced to the world that he had discovered the Scaean Gate and the Palace of Priam. Comfortable in their well-appointed studies, enclosed by walls of books rather than ancient stonework, scholars rejected his claims and attacked his methods. Unperturbed by this academic vituperation and the obtuseness of both Turkish and Greek officials, Schliemann published his own view in *Trojan Antiquities*. 'If people are disappointed in their expectations', he wrote, 'and consider that Troy was too small for the great deeds of the *Iliad*, and that Homer exaggerated everything with a poet's freedom, they must, on the other hand, find a great satisfaction in the certainty now established that the Homeric poems are based on actual facts.' He also turned his attention to another site, Mycenae, the stronghold of Agamemnon, who had led the Achaean forces against Troy.

According to Pausanias, whose *Guidebook to Greece* was written about 170, at the site of Mycenae 'parts of the wall are still preserved as well as the gate over which the lions stand. In the ruins there is . . . the tomb of Agamemnon, one of Eurymedon the charioteer, and one of Teledamus and Pelops – for they say Cassandra gave birth to these twins and that while they were still infants Aegisthus killed them with the parents – and one of Electra . . . . Clytemnestra and Aegisthus were buried a little outside the

wall, for they were not deemed worthy of burial within it, where Agememnon lies and those who were murdered with him.' Schliemann was determined to find these burial places when he began his digging in 1876.

Once again the seeker of the Homeric world was not the first excavator to have tried the site. Lord Elgin had already removed part of the pillared entrance belonging to the Treasury of Atreus, an impressively vaulted circular tomb. But careful reading of Pausanias and good luck assisted Schliemann in unearthing the graves inside the Lion Gate. Hard by this entrance he struck upon a circular enclosure, some 24 metres in diameter, containing grave-stones sculptured with scenes of hunting and battle. Here he was sure reposed the mortal remains of Agamemnon. Further excava-tion revealed the presence of six shaft-graves and within these ancient tombs were the bones of nineteen people, many of whom were decked with gold. The golden breast plate and death mask of one of these warriors persuaded Schliemann that, as he tele-graphed the King of Greece, he had 'gazed upon the face of Agamemnon'.

Just as he had uncovered 'windy Troy' where the *Iliad* had suggested to him that it might be, so the great archaeologist had succeeded in discovering 'golden Mycenae'. Scholars were obliged to admit that Schliemann had a case. But what he had discovered, we now understand, were the relics of some five hundred or more years of civilization in Mycenae, ending in about 1150 BC.

Above left: Heinrich Schliemann addressing the Society of Antiquaries at Burlington House. After the dis-coveries at Mycenae, scholars were obliged to take his work seriously

Above: Mrs Schliemann wearing the golden jewellery excavated at Mycenae.

Arthur Evans believed that the Mycenaean finds were far older than the Trojan War and may have told Schliemann as much on their meeting in Athens in 1882. However, it is likely that he concentrated upon the jewellery, especially the engraved beads and signet rings. These artefacts puzzled him greatly. Whilst they seemed to recall Mesopotamian and Egyptian gems, there was a quality that suggested an Aegean provenance. The octopus design for instance. Evans wondered about the antecedents of Mycenaean civilization. In the meantime Schliemann continued his archaeological quest, and after working at Tiryns, south of Mycenae, as well as Orchomenos, to the north in Boeotia, he sought permission to dig on the island of Crete. Problems over the purchase of the site at Knossos discouraged this venture and so it was not until 1900, after the end of Turkish rule, that excavations started under the direction of Evans, not Schliemann.

Sir Arthur Evans

Having looked at the tiny engravings on the Mycenaean finds, Evans encountered similar designs on small lens-shaped stones in an Athens antique shop. He realized that they were seals and recognized in some cases hieroglyphic signs. When the dealer said they came from Crete, Evans set off to inquire into this early form of writing. On the island he learned that Cretan women valued the seal-stones as charms – they were known as 'milk stones' – and from his own observations he felt that 'the golden age of Crete lies far beyond the limits of the historical period'. It was an intuition proved correct at Knossos, where he started excavating in 1900. As he noted in the initial month there, the workers turned up 'nothing Greek – nothing Roman . . . . Nay, its great period goes at least well back to the pre-Mycenaean period'. Evans had located the major site of Europe's earliest civilization.

The excavation of the Palace of Minos at Knossos was a more formidable task than anyone had expected. The labyrinthine ruins were so extensive that Evans decided to make it his life's work. In 1906 he built the Villa Ariadne to serve as a permanent headquarters for the excavation, and in 1909 he resigned as Keeper of the Ashmolean Museum at Oxford. Three years later he was knighted for his contribution to learning. Archaeological activity at Knossos was continuous from 1900 till 1914 and 1920 till 1932: the cost of this to Evans' private fortune was probably £250,000.

In the early stages of digging Evans held to his belief that the prehistoric script was the most important discovery. On 5 April 1900 he excitedly reported 'an entire hoard of these clay documents, many of them perfect, was discovered midst a deposit of charred wood in a bath-shaped receptacle of terracotta set close against the wall'. Additional finds of inscriptions allowed the publication of *Scripta Minoa* in 1909, but as more and more of the palace was uncovered his priority became its description and preservation. The first fresco had been also unearthed on 5 April: it was the famous Cup-bearer, carrying a rhyton, or high, funnel-shaped cup. Evans was reminded 'of the figures on Etruscan tombs and the *Keftiu* of Egyptian paintings'. Then on 13 April he found 'the Council Chamber of Minos', the Throne Room. In his diary Evans noted:

The chief event of the day was the result of the continued excavation of the bath chamber. The parapet of the bath proved to have another circular cutting at its east end, and as this was filled with charred wood – cypress – these openings were evidently for columns. On the other side of the north wall was a short bench like that of the outer chamber, and then separated from it by a small interval a separate seat of honour or Throne. It had a high back, like the seat, of gypsum, which was partly embedded in the stucco wall. It was raised on a square base and had a curious moulding below with crockets (almost Gothic).

Other rooms soon came to light along with their amazing frescoes. In 1907 and 1908 he not only continued to dig out the Palace of Minos but also uncovered the Little Palace. It was clear that at Knossos there had flourished a great palace city whose origins went back to the rude settlements of the Neolithic period. Evans reckoned habitation began as early as 6000 BC, and this guess has now been confirmed by radiocarbon dating. Knossos is the oldest Neolithic settlement in Europe.

Not lost on the excavators was the connection between Knossos and Mycenae. The magnificent golden head of a bull found by Schliemann in the shaft-graves appeared to echo the Minoan obsession with that animal. That the extensive Central Court of the Palace of Minos was the scene of bull games there could be little doubt after they discovered the bull-leaping fresco. Evans marvelled:

The girl acrobat in front seizes the horns of a coursing bull at full gallop, one of which seems to run under her left armpit. The object of her grip clearly seems to be to gain a purchase for a backward somersault over the animal's back, such as is being performed by the boy. The second female performer behind stretches out both her hands as if to catch the flying figure or at least to steady him when he comes to earth the right way up.

Of all known illustrations of the bull games this is the only one showing all parts of the contest. What strikes the observer today, as it must have done in Minoan times, is the dramatic contrast bet-ween the unbridled power of the beast and the vulnerable supple-ness of the toreadors. Acrobatic skill, not bronze weapons, ensured a successful performance. In this amazing ritual, Evans wondered, had they chanced upon the source of the Athenian tribute of youths and maidens to be sacrificed each year to the Minotaur in the Theseus myth. 'What a part these creatures play here! On the frescoes and reliefs, the chief design of the seals, on a steatite vase, above the gate it may be of the Palace itself. Was not some one or other of these creatures visible on the ruined site in the early Dorian days, which gave the actual tradition of the Bull of Minos?'

Knossos had been iden-
tified as a probable site
in the 1880s, but it was
not until Crete gained
its independence in
1898 that Sir Arthur
Evans was able to buy
the necessary land.
Excavations started in
1900 and it soon became
clear that a new chapter
in archaeology
had begun.

Above left: One of the
most exciting dis-
coveries during the first
season of digging was
the Throne Room

Above: Sir Arthur Evans (in the white helmet) and a companion supervising the clearing of the site

Right: One of the shrines discovered in the palace. Horns of consecration and an offering tray can be seen

Opposite bottom: The scene in the West Magazine after the first stage of clearance showing how a large number of the pithoi remained virtually intact

An architectural feature which impressed Evans was the Grand Staircase, explored for the first time in 1901. 'It is evident', he wrote, 'that we are only just coming to the real centre of the Palace buildings. We have now a hall with two column-bases approached by a quadruple flight of stairs.' The excavation of the stairway presented many hindrances and hazards. 'The hewing away of the clay concretions and the extraction of the various rubble and earthy materials of the intervening spaces left a void between the upper and lower spaces that threatened the collapse of the whole. The carbonized posts and beams and shafts, although their form and measurement could be often observed, were splintered up and exposed and, of course, could afford no support. The recourse to mine props and miscellaneous timbering was almost temporary and at times so insufficient that some dangerous falls occurred.' Various alternatives were tried but it was not until the 1920s that reinforced concrete provided a sure method of saving the complex structure. Then the original 'timber framework' of huge posts and column shafts, a singular way of supporting the successive levels, was replaced by a 'reinforced concrete restoration'.

In *The Palace of Minos* Evans summed up the result in these words:

The Grand Staircase, as thus reconstituted, stands alone among ancient architectural remains. With its charred columns solidly restored in their pristine hues, surrounding in tiers its central walls, its balustrades rising, practically intact, one above the other, with its imposing fresco of great Minoan shields on the back wall of its middle gallery now replaced in replica, and its still well-preserved gypsum steps ascending to four landings, it revives, as no other part of the building, the remote past.

Part of the elaborate drainage system which was built at Knossos

Another feature of the palace design which persuaded Evans of the advanced nature of Minoan civilization was the plumbing. The inhabitants at Knossos did not rely on wells alone but were supplied with running water brought in via tightly cemented terracotta piping. This pressure system may have been fed by water in the surrounding hills, as revealed in the discovery of a conduit heading towards the palace from a nearby spring. To deal with rainwater and waste the Minoans constructed a network of drains, the one serving the Central Court being a sizeable channel built of stone and lined with cement. Air-shafts and manholes indicated the inhabitants' concern for hygiene and health. The underground drains were places 'so roomy that my Cretan workmen spent whole days in them without inconvenience. The elaborate drainage system of the Palace and the connected sanitary arrangements excite the wonder of all beholders. The terracotta pipes, with their scientifically-shaped sections, nicely interlocked, which date from the earliest days of the building, are quite up to modern standards.'

In 1928 Evans presented the site of Knossos to the British School at Athens, and from this date excavations were conducted by its officials. One of these was John Pendlebury, who published in 1939 *The Archaeology of Crete* as an attempt to survey the culture of the island from the prehistoric period to the Roman occupation. In this book he addressed himself to the destruction of Minoan Crete and pictured Theseus leading a band of Achaean warriors intent on throwing off the yoke of the Sea-King. So it was:

. . . in the last decade of the fifteenth century on a spring day, when a strong south wind was blowing which carried the flames of the burning beams horizontally northwards, Knossos fell.

The final scene takes place in the most dramatic room ever excavated – the Throne Room. It was found in a state of complete confusion. A great oil jar lay overturned in one corner, ritual vessels were in the act of being used when the disaster came. It looks as if the king had been hurried here to undergo too late some last ceremony in the hopes of saving the people. Theseus and the Minotaur! Dare we believe that he wore the mask of a bull?

The Psychro Cave

A critic of the 'reconstitutions' undertaken by Evans at Knossos was D. G. Hogarth, Director of the British School in Athens. His opposition to such 'expensive methods' and his reluctance to allow public subscriptions to be used in a 'princely' way compelled Evans to provide the funds himself. Although the two archaeologists did co-operate in opening up the site, the difference of opinion encouraged Hogarth to look elsewhere, and in 1900 he excavated the Psychro Cave on the heights of Lasithi. It was a spectacular expedition: from the undisturbed lower grotto he recovered hundreds of votive offerings in bronze, lead, gold, terracotta, and

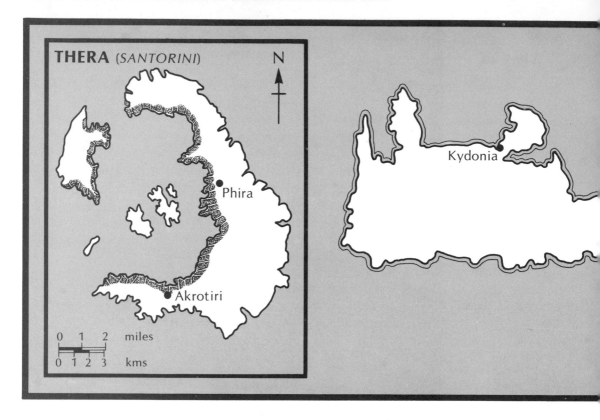

precious stones. The Psychro Cave has a strong claim to be the Dictaean Cave, the birthplace of Zeus according to later Greek tradition. Hogarth believed firmly that its fantastic stalactites and icy pool were a 'fit scene for Minos' mysterious colloquy with his father Zeus, and the after-cult of a Chthonian god'.

The Psychro Cave was accidentally discovered by peasants in 1883, and was explored by several archaeologists. Evans dug there in 1896, but only four years afterwards did a thorough excavation take place, when Hogarth arrived 'with a few trained men, stone-hammers, mining-bars, blasting powder, and the rest of a digger's plant'. The cave was divided into two parts: an upper and a lower grotto, entry to the latter being obstructed by boulders which had tumbled down from the roof. Having shifted these rocks without causing further falls, Hogarth directed his workmen to 'the abysmal chasm' beyond. Here they encountered a forest of stalactites overhanging a subterranean lake: this was the ancient sanctuary, the inner shrine, a repository over 3,000 years old; everywhere they looked were votive offerings wedged into crevices – double axes, daggers, ornaments, and statuettes. The sight of 'these pillared halls of unknown extent and abysmal gloom' moved Hogarth to declare that their religious function did 'honour to the primitive Cretan imagination'. It was but an acknowledgement of the archetype of the Minoan pillar crypt.

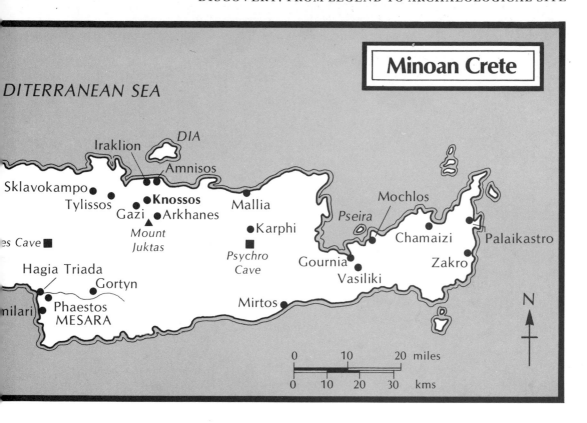

Phaestos and Hagia Triada

Reporting in September 1906 the progress of archaeology in an article written for *The Illustrated London News* Hogarth recalled:

Crete has made no small noise in the whole of recent years, and not so much by its modern developments as by its antiquities. Long the least known archaeologically of all the great Mediterranean islands, it was no sooner opened to research by the establishment of autonomy than it proved a veritable mine of things old and strange. Now that the fact is proved, one sees how suitable the island must have been for the evolution of a high civilization in early times, with its wide plains, high rain-condensing mountains, and long seaboards; the whole set in a singularly favourable geographical position; but no one had more than a dim suspicion of the truth till Mr. Arthur Evans began to lift the veil. Fortunately, more ancient treasures still lay underground in Crete than in any other Greek land. Ever since the Western World began to concern itself about antiquities, this island has been too stormy a spot for treasure-hunters. Christian and Moslem, and even Christians Latin and Orthodox, have fought above the palaces and graves of more civilized predecessors without being able to spare time or thought to them. Thus the British, Italian, and American scholars, waiting till 1900, had the chance of a century.

They have used it to the full, the British at Knossos, near Candia, in the Cave of Psychro, and at Praesos, Palaikastro and Zakro in Eastern Crete; the Italians at Phaestos and Hagia Triada in the south centre; and the Americans at Gournia on the Bay of Mirabello . . . .

Above: The northern end
of the Central Court
at Phaestos

The Italian Mission, under Professor F. Halbherr, has opened out a
great palace crowning a bluff near the ancient Phaestos and commanding
the broad plain of Mesara. In size and interest it is inferior to the
Knossian, but in spectacular effect superior, being more easily seen at
once, and, in some respects, better preserved. Moreover it is set in much
finer natural surroundings. Its main components are a great central court,
on which open the living rooms; a great stairway to the *megaron*, flanked
by a stepped area like that at Knossos; and a western court and plinth of
the palace platform. About two miles west of this palace Professor
Halbherr hit upon another site of great interest near the little church of
the Holy Trinity (Hagia Triada). Here the remains of a princely villa
have been preserved by the *talus* of a hill, and the room still contained
objects of extraordinary value. Two steatite cups, with scenes sculptured
in relief, found there rank with the finest 'Aegean' art-treasures yet
discovered; and a painted sarcophagus, brought to light in a neighbouring cemetery, is a priceless record and monument of the religious beliefs

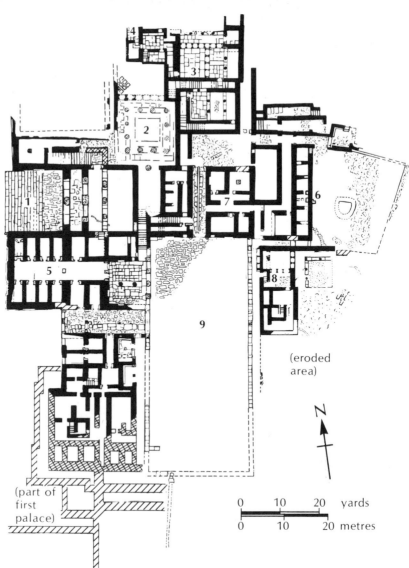

of the early Cretans. The internal frescoes of the villa were also of singular beauty and interest.

To Evans 'the Patriarch of Cretan excavation' was the Italian, Frederico Halbherr, who arrived in 1884. Together with a local archaeologist, Joseph Hazzidakis, he had prospected for ancient sites and recovered from peasants near the Psychro Cave the first Minoan antiquities. In 1866 the site of the palace at Phaestos was identified and its eventual excavation, along with the ruins of Hagia Triada, fell to Haibherr and his colleagues.

Of the Minoan palaces which have been discovered so far on Crete, Phaestos gives the best idea of what the earliest palaces were like, since later building there was not always directly on top of existing remains. In many places the outlines of the first rooms dating from 2000 to 1700 BC are discernible, except on the eastern

51

side of the central courtyard where erosion has altered the slope of the hill. When the palace at Phaestos was destroyed by earthquake about 1700 BC a new one was constructed, but after the sack of 1450 BC this too was abandoned. There is reason to believe that Knossos was the model followed, not least because the name of Phaestos occurs in inscriptions found there and the similarity of general ground-plans. A notable architectural feature at Phaestos was the imposing Grand Staircase leading from the West Court into the main entrance of the palace. It seems less aptly termed a theatral area than the one at the end of the Royal Road in Knossos. Situated in the West Court were some of the cult rooms belonging to the old palace and many traces of cooking suggest that the eating of offerings by participants happened in Minoan rituals.

The entrance hall itself ended in a light-well and three small doorways. One of these doors led by a circuitous passage to a small open space, the Peristyle Court, which had four columns on each side, or offered access to a staircase connected with the upper storey; another took the visitor near the storerooms and onto the Central Court; the last door was for the guardroom. The lack of an impressive doorway to match the Grand Staircase is reminiscent of the indirectness used in the design of Knossos. The magazines and cult rooms were also to the west of the Central Court but, unlike the Palace of Minos, here the private rooms of the royal family were placed in the northern wing, presumably to allow an uninterrupted view of the Psiloriti Mountains. Yet the verandah used for this breathcatching view adjoined a three-chambered room like the Hall of the Double Axes and it is probable that it was used for similar purposes. In the eastern wing, to the south of the usual workshops, a self-contained set of rooms existed possibly for distinguished guests, but the disappearance of other buildings on the eroded hillside leaves the use of this whole section in doubt.

The most fascinating find on the site is the so-called Phaestos Disc, which was discovered in 1908 among the ruins of the northeastern part of the old palace. It is a disc of fired clay, about 15mm in diameter, impressed on both sides with picture writing. Ever since then the disc has been the centre of academic controversy, including numerous attempts at decipherment. In the next chapter we shall discuss the recent interpretation of the Bulgarian linguist Vladimir Georgiev, who argues that the inscription is a report in Luvian addressed to the king of Phaestos. Luvian was a language spoken in many parts of Asia Minor in the second millennium BC.

A half hour's walk from Phaestos is the royal villa and settlement at Hagia Triada. The Minoan name remains unknown and so the neighbouring church of Holy Trinity supplies its rather odd designation. It is a difficult site to understand. Not only were there two periods of habitation, accompanied by much remodelling and rebuilding, but even the official publication of its excavation has not yet appeared.

Opposite above: A view across the West Court at Phaestos showing the Grand Staircase

Opposite below: The workshops at Phaestos which lie on the eastern side of the palace

Left: Looking south-west across the villa at Hagia Triada towards the sea

Right: Part of the elaborate drainage system at the villa

Before 1550 BC Hagia Triada comprised little more than a collection of houses. But about that date a magnificent villa was built, and connected by a paved road with the palace at Phaestos. The substantial village adjoining the northern wing may have been established at the same time to meet its needs. An aspect of the Minoan site was the presence of the sea, which then came right up to the foot of the villa ridge. Hagia Triada could have served as the summer residence of the rulers of Phaestos. It was constructed on the grand scale, gypsum veneering being lavishly used throughout, and the frescoes are among the finest examples known. As can be seen from the plan, the villa forms an irregular L, rather like half a palace. The open area enclosed by the L was partly flagged, and

Above: The North and
West Wings of the villa
at Hagia Triada

**The villa at
Hagia Triada**

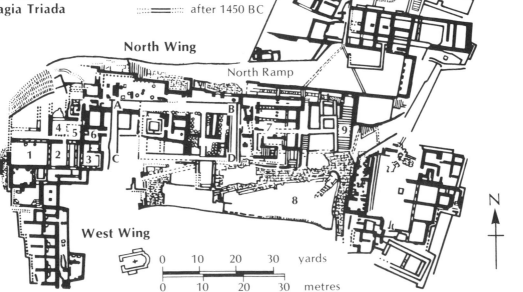

1 Reception Hall
2 Courtyard
3 Drawing-room
4 Archive
5 Room with
   frescoes
6 Storeroom
7 State Apartments
8 Sanctuary
9 Steps to
   North Ramp
10 Shops

A B C D Megaron

:::::::▬▬▬▬::::::: before 1450 BC

::::::═══:::::: after 1450 BC

Village

North Wing

North Ramp

West Wing

0   10   20   30   yards

0   10   20   30   metres

N

stood on the crest of the ridge into whose slopes the first-floor rooms were terraced. The long northern wing contained the living quarters of the royal family, while the short western wing was filled with workshops, storerooms, and accommodation for servants. In one of the rooms at the junction of the L the archaeologists found an archive of clay tablets inscribed with Linear A, the oldest form of Cretan linear script.

The villa and the village were destroyed about 1450 BC. Shortly afterwards the village rose again from the cinders, but not until 1200 BC was anything erected on the ruins of the royal residence. This new building took the form of a Mycenaean *megaron*, a hall that probably served a religious purpose in connection with an open-air sanctuary. Unearthed were large numbers of votive offerings such as terracotta bulls.

Harriet Boyd

In 1900 a resourceful American lady named Harriet Boyd enlisted the support of Evans and Hogarth in getting permission to excavate in Crete. At Evans' suggestion she looked into a group of Iron Age tombs on the southern shore of Mirabello Bay, and while excavating them she became convinced that there had once been a Bronze Age settlement somewhere in the vicinity. At the end of the digging session she travelled to Iraklion with her Greek foreman and his mother, who acted as a chaperone, and set about preparing for a search of the area in the following year.

News of her interest in Minoan ruins spread so widely during the winter that local peasants were able to indicate the likely spot on her return. Close by the sea at Gournia her team of workmen in 1901 cut down trees, cleared away scrub, and dug trial trenches. She was amazed by the results of the first day's work!

Our astonishment when we reached Gournia was indeed great. The men scattered over the hillside were in high spirits, for had not Lysimachus produced the first good find of the season – a perfect bronze spear point, and Michael Paviadhakis, a curved bronze knife buried scarcely a foot below the surface? One man after another called us to see potsherds, fragments of stone vases, etc. he had saved for our inspection. Perhaps the proudest workman was he who had laid bare a well-paved road, the threshold of a house and a small clay gutter. Everything pointed to a prehistoric settlement of some importance, whose existence on that site had remained unsuspected until that day. Such a discovery could not fail to appeal to the imagination of the peasants. We had no difficulty in getting new hands and began work the next morning with fifty men almost as eager as ourselves.

Within three days we had opened houses, were following paved roads, and had in our possession enough vases and sherds bearing octopus, ivy-leaf, double axe and other unmistakably Minoan designs as well as bronze tools, seal impressions, stone vases, etc., to make certain that we had found what we were seeking, a Bronze Age settlement of the best period of Cretan civilization.

Shrine

Palace

Public
Court

N

| 0 | 10 | 20 | 30 | yards |
| 0 | 10 | 20 | 30 | metres |

Above: The plan of
Gournia which shows the
compact nature of the site

Opposite above: Looking
down the hillside at
Gournia showing the
small houses and narrow
streets of the town

Opposite below:
A terracotta container
from Gournia which was
possibly a bath

In three years Harriet Boyd, with two female companions, made
Gournia the most excavated Minoan town. Her own account of the
site was published in 1908.

Perched on the north end of a small ridge, Gournia was inhabited as early as 3000 BC, though there was no settlement of any
importance till about 1650 BC when a town grew up, ruled by a
prince or governor who lived in a diminutive palace. The destruction of 1450 BC was visited upon the town and only parts of it were
briefly reoccupied afterwards. In its heyday Gournia was the
centre of industrious activities; its people were farmers, fishermen,
weavers, bronze-casters, potters, and carpenters.

Although the palace was ten times smaller than Knossos, its
poorly-preserved remains indicate that it shared certain basic
characteristics. There was a tiny western courtyard, a series of
magazines for storing foodstuffs, a main west entrance, and to the

south a large open space, called by Harriet Boyd a Public Court. This could have been used for bull games because within a short columned entrance on the western side were situated two small rooms not unlike pillar crypts. Nearby lay a huge flat stone slab, 2.75m square and 0.23m thick, pierced by a large hole from top to bottom. Perhaps this was an altar stone on which the bull was sacrificed after the ritual contests.

In the middle of the town, to the north of the palace, was a shrine consisting of a single room without a porch. Inside was found a terracotta idol of a snake-entwined goddess with raised hands, together with fragments of other clay statues. It has been argued plausibly that such shrines were only introduced to Crete in the final stage of Minoan civilization.

Mallia and Zakro

Excluding the governor's residence at Gournia, archaeologists have to date located four Minoan palaces. Whereas the palatial buildings at Knossos and Phaestos were dug by foreigners, those at Mallia, 40 kilometres east of Iraklion, and Zakro, on the eastern end of the island, were detected by Greek scholars. In 1915 Joseph Hazzidakis commenced the excavation of the Mallia palace, which was about the size of Phaestos, and in 1962 Nicolas Platon, with financial aid from the United States, started work at Zakro.

Though less elegant than either Knossos or Phaestos, Mallia was in its overall plan much the same, apart from a few individual peculiarities. Notable effects were the porticoes along the northern

Left: The *kernos* at Mallia which may have served as an altar for offerings of fruit and seeds

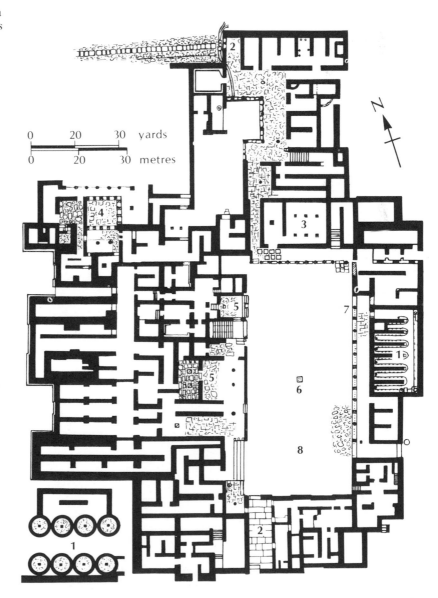

The palace at Mallia

1 Magazines
2 Entrances
3 Kitchen
4 Domestic Quarters
5 Cult Rooms
6 Altar
7 Post holes
8 Central Court

and eastern sides of the Central Court. The remains of a balustrade in the spaces between the columns gave the clue to use of the open area for bull games; safely behind this screen people would have been able to watch the performances. In the middle of the Central Court there was set up an altar stone, but the most interesting religious find occurred near the Grand Staircase, where stood a *kernos*, a large disc-shaped stone with a circular depression in the centre and smaller depressions round the rim. It may have served as an altar for offerings of fruit and seeds. The storage facilities for grain were enhanced by the construction of eight *koulouras* in the south-west corner of the palace. These circular pits were not so deep as those at Knossos, but their central pillars have survived to indicate that each once possessed a beehive roof.

The ancient name for Mallia is not known. A strong contender would be Milatos, whose colony on the Carian shore of Asia Minor was Miletos. The first palace there was put up about 2000 BC and badly damaged three centuries later by an earthquake: its successor was consumed by fire in 1450 BC. A similar pattern of construction and destruction has been revealed at Zakro.

In 1894 Evans had told Hogarth of the natural port at Zakro, 'the last on the directest sea-route from the Aegean to the Cyrenaic shore'. As a result of this prompting Hogarth undertook an excavation seven years later, and proved the site to be a rich Minoan settlement, but he missed the palace there. Not until 1962 did the spade of an archaeologist disclose the outline of a small, though fine, palatial building. Its excavation holds much promise for our understanding of Minoan life because Zakro was not reoccupied or even looted after the great catastrophe of 1450 BC.

The interconnection of the economy and religion is already demonstrated in the south-west corner of the palace. In close proximity were a shrine, an archive, a storeroom, a workshop, and

The treasury and shrine complex in the palace at Zakro

a treasury, which had nine chests built of mud brick with plaster floors. These chests were filled with remarkable cups, vases, statues, and ornaments.

Minoans overseas

The three hundred years preceding 1450 BC saw the zenith of Minoan civilization. Crete was densely populated: it was Homer's 'rich and lovely land . . . boasting ninety cities'. Overpopulation may have been a problem because, like the later Greeks, the Minoans had already sent out colonists overseas. Settlements on two Aegean islands, Kythera and Thera, throw considerable light on the Minoans.

Before 2000 BC a colony was founded at Kastri on the island of Kythera between the western tip of Crete and the Peloponnese. An Anglo-American excavation conducted in the 1960s uncovered a Bronze Age town and dug a number of tombs. It established that the site was continuously occupied till 1450 BC and that at its close was a prosperous Minoan outpost, possibly in contact with Pylos and the south-western Peloponnese. Most of the finds were Cretan in origin, being imports from the island, though in the final years a slight Mycenaean influence appeared. Kastri was abandoned, not destroyed: possibly the colonists decided to leave rather than submit when Knossos fell to the invading Mycenaeans.

Thera, modern Santorini, a volcanic island about 100 kilometres north of Crete, was once an important Minoan satellite, though not perhaps a colony. In its present form it is a submerged crater of a volcano, the remains of a gigantic eruption. The island comprises a deep layer of volcanic ash overlaying pumice and the original rock. When the building of the Suez Canal began in 1859, the Santorini ash was mined for the production of cement, and incidentally stone foundations came to notice there. Archaeologists uncovered frescoes and masonry of a fine quality, but it was not till 1967 that the Greek scholar Spiridon Marinatos made his famous finds at Akrotiri. He identified Minoan frescoes of flowers, birds, monkeys, antelopes, and a pair of youthful boxers. Then he brought to light a fresco of a landscape, possibly in Libya. There was a strong local flavour to some of the designs, a characteristic also of the pottery, but it should be regarded as a variation within the Minoan tradition.

The absence of skeletons lends weight to the argument that the inhabitants of Thera got sufficient warning to leave the island with their treasures. A severe earthquake was probably the signal. This occurred about 1500 BC and the subsequent eruption, one of the most stupendous in history, evidently wrought havoc on Crete. Earth tremors, huge waves, and a blanket of ash: these afflicted the Minoans, whose civilization was severely damaged in the disaster.

3

Who were
the Minoans?

'Nothing Greek – Nothing Roman'

The settlement of Crete is a puzzle which has not yet been completely solved. Evans was correct in his estimate of the pre-
Mycenaean age of Knossos, a site inhabited for several millennia
even before the construction of palatial buildings, but the choice of
the term Minoan to describe the Bronze Age period on the island
was somewhat misleading in that it conveyed an impression of
cultural and ethnic homogeneity. It must be said, however, that he
did suggest as the impetus of Minoan civilization the arrival of
refugees from Libya. These people would have quit the area
adjacent to the Nile delta region when this was conquered by
Mena, who according to tradition united northern and southern
Egypt around 3000 BC. Affinities were the codpiece and the
custom of leaving locks of hair hanging down in front of the ears.
But a similar piece of clothing to the straight codpiece appears on
early Egyptian figurines. In Libya and Crete therefore the cod-
piece as well as the forelock may represent survivals of fashions
once general throughout the eastern Mediterranean. Such
evidence is too slender to argue that Minoan stock as a whole was of
Libyan origin.

On the Mesara Plain, the domain of the rulers of Phaestos, are
the remains of ancient circular tombs. These were communal,
used for generations by a clan or a family. Although the Libyans
built circular tombs, the Cretan ones are not strictly comparable,
since the problem of their roofing is complicated. None have survived with a roof, and it is sometimes argued that they were
either open-air enclosures or had flat roofs like Minoan houses.
They were built above ground, and had their floors sunk only a
metre below it. The circular tombs and the custom of collective
burial were probably a development of Neolithic customs.

The Greek Legends

Before discussing the four different scripts employed at various
times in Bronze Age Crete so as to establish the language or
languages spoken then, we need to review the few Greek traditions

A woman from one of the fine Minoan frescoes found on Thera

about the Minoans. The earliest information on the inhabitants of the island is contained in the *Odyssey*. According to Homer, the peoples of Crete were the Achaeans, Eteocretans, Kydonians, Dorians, and Pelasgians. Many scholars have contested the authenticity of this list because of the reference to the Dorians, whose name occurs nowhere else in the *Odyssey* or *Iliad*. They argue that the list, or at least the name of the Dorians, is a late interpolation. It would seem, however, that the poet accurately reflects the ethnic situation of Crete after the Dorian invasion, which Thucydides placed later than 1120 BC. The Mycenaean Greeks, or Achaeans, had occupied Knossos about 1450 BC and for a number of years held most of the islanders in subjection. Having overwhelmed Mycenae and the other cities of their brother-Greeks eighty years after the Trojan War, the Dorians crossed from the Peloponnese to Crete. The Pelasgians, an Aegean people whose tongue was probably a language intermediate between Thracian and Hittite-Luvian, may have come from Thessaly – a tradition Andron of Halikarnassos recorded in the fourth century BC. The Kydonians, settled at the western end of the island, derived their name from a town or city meaning 'illustrious'. This Greek derivation has tempted several scholars to identify them as Greek-speaking but another interpretation would see the Kydonians as Luvians, a people from south-western Asia Minor. Lastly, the Eteocretans, 'true Cretans', were perhaps the survivors of the early Minoan people.

The *Iliad* provides a catalogue of the contingents sent to the Trojan War. The Cretan fleet of eighty ships was commanded by Meriones and Idomeneus, 'grandson of Minos', its crews drawn 'from Knossos, from Gortys of the great walls, from Lyctos, Miletos, chalky Lycastos, Phaestos, and Rhytion, fine cities all of them; and the other troops that had their homes in Crete of the hundred towns'. From the smallness of the fleet, only equal in size to that led by the lord of Tiryns, we can gauge the collapse of the island's reputation as a naval power. The disastrous expedition to Sicily could have been the cause. A Minos – whether Minoan or Greek – met his doom at Kamikos, where he had gone to look for the architect Daedalus. The armada sent to avenge the death of the king was obliged to abandon a siege and suffered shipwreck on the return voyage. After this reverse Crete was the prey of adventurers, though some of the destruction wrought on the island must be attributed to the Minoans in their efforts to topple intruding Mycenaean princes. The political scene was very different to that found in the Theseus myth. In killing the Minotaur the Athenian prince succeeded in removing the burden of tribute from his state, but there is no suggestion of more than a temporary scuttling of Minoan power. Theseus coincided with the decline, not the fall, of Minos' authority.

A final legend of note turns on Minoan connections with Asia Minor. Herodotus reported that the Termilians of Lycia believed themselves to be descendants of colonists who had come to Asia Minor with Sarpedon from Crete. About 1600 BC the king of Knossos expelled Sarpedon from Cretan Milatos, whence the fugitive moved to the Asian coast and founded Miletos. If the Termilians descended from those who accompanied him did not change their language completely later on, then the implication is that an early form of the Lycian tongue was current on Crete. Termilian, or Lycian, is a Luvian dialect.

Hieroglyphic and Linear A

Four scripts existed at different times and places on Bronze Age Crete. They were an early hieroglyphic form associated with seal-stones; two linear scripts largely preserved on clay tablets which have been hardened during the burning down of buildings – Evans called the older script recognized throughout Minoan sites 'Linear Class A' to distinguish it from 'Linear Class B', the script in use at Knossos at the time of the final destruction of the palace in the fourteenth century BC or somewhat later; and the picture-like signs, printed with wooden stamps, on the spiral inscription of the clay Phaestos Disc.

The art of writing, as well as that of seal engraving, may have been introduced from Syria about the third millennium BC. Disturbances in that region caused by the arrival of invaders from Asia Minor could have encouraged overseas migration, though it is by no means uncertain that the idea of engraving was simply imported to meet local needs. A quickening of Cretan civilization was then taking place. The earliest evidence for writing in Crete is on stone seals and their clay impressions. These signs Evans named the Hieroglyphic or Pictographic, and noted resemblances between some of them and the oldest Egyptian script. In *Scripta Minoa* and in contributions to learned journals, he argued that pictographs were once widely diffused. Their 'development from the simple pictographic to the hieroglyphic or quasi-alphabetic might naturally be expected to have taken place in more than one European area had it not been cut short by the invasion of the fully-equipped Phoenician system of writing'. Although the

One of the baked-clay tablets with Linear A script found at Hagia Triada

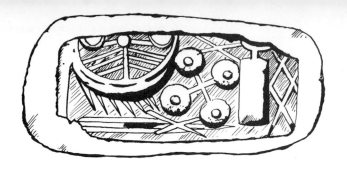

A drawing of clay sealing which Evans suggested means 'export oil'

notion of a single system of writing developed at an early period in the Aegean is now discarded, the discovery of comparable signs on pottery in Romania, Troy, Melos, Thessaly, Cyprus, and Egypt supposes a widespread acquaintance with writing if not the use of it. Most likely is the theory that the first spread of writing or of signs derived from it may have taken place in religious context. Writing was probably copied for magical purposes, often perhaps without it being understood.

Evans made an analysis of the subjects traced in the hieroglyphs. His main categories were the human body and its parts; arms, implements, and instruments; cult objects and symbols; houses and enclosures; utensils, stores, and treasure; ships and marine objects; animals and their parts; insects; plants and trees; sky and earth; uncertain objects and geometrical signs. From the information thus collected he was able to sketch Minoan civilization as it was at the end of the third millennium BC, but except in one instance he could give no explanation of how the hieroglyphic script worked. His single interpretation was of a clay sealing, whose impression showed an olive-spray and a ship. This, Evans proffered, meant 'export oil'.

Hieroglyphic script was succeeded at Phaestos and Knossos before 1700 BC by a linear script, which seems to have developed from it. The first volume of *The Palace of Minos at Knossos*, published in 1921, contains a section entitled 'Linear Script A and its Sacral Usage'. Here Evans commented on the restricted use of Linear B, detected only on clay tablets at Knossos, whereas Linear A was employed also for inscriptions on other objects, and especially those with a religious function.

Linear A appears to have been written in the language of the Eteocretans, the 'true Cretans'. By 1600 BC it was used by scribes over a large part of the island, though tablets are rare except at Hagia Triada. Evans' observation about the frequency of Linear A in dedications is still valid. Archaeology has turned up nothing to dislodge the older linear script from its position as the tongue of the priest-kings. On the contrary there is reason to look upon Linear B as an intruder into Crete from mainland Greece.

Finds of baked clay tablets in the ruins of Phaestos and Hagia Triada have led scholars to the view that hieroglyphic and linear scripts overlapped to an unexpected extent. Linear A doubtless evolved from Hieroglyphic, as Evans thought, but we can no longer assume a change-over shortly after 1800 BC, since in early deposits at Phaestos transitional signs indicate that a proto-linear script already existed. Inscriptions in Linear A are few and a good many are damaged. Although there is no agreement as to the language inscribed, several scholars have put forward interesting interpretations. In 1958 Leonard Palmer showed that a recurrent word in Linear A inscriptions, *asasara, asasarame*, corresponds to the Hittite *ishassara-s*, 'mistress'. The Babylonian Ishtar, who became the foremost of the Hittite goddesses, was commonly dignified by the title 'My Lady'. In Luvian, a language closely related to Hittite and spoken in the parts of Asia Minor nearest to Crete, the title of 'My Lady' would have been *asha-saras-mes*. Palmer later translated an inscription on a libation table found at Knossos as Luvian for: 'This altar erects for My Lady. No one shall take offerings from it.' What he was seeking to do by this translation was to show that *asasara*, unlike the title of *Madonna* today, could not be discounted as a religious loan-word. His interpretation that in matters of worship the Minoans and the Luvians had something in common is now challenged, despite archaeological evidence from Beycesultan, an important Luvian centre in Asia Minor. A shrine discovered there consisted of two upright clay stelae, originally more than 1 metre high, the gap being emphasized in front by clay horns resembling Minoan horns of consecration. Beycesultan was destroyed in the eighteenth century BC by the Hittites, who were then extending their authority eastwards into the Arzawa lands. Before this event, Palmer argues, the Luvians had already reached Greece.

Vladimir Georgiev, the Bulgarian philologist whose recent decipherment of the Phaestos Disc we shall turn to shortly, holds that two languages were set down in Linear A. According to Georgiev, one of them was an ancient form of Greek, the tongue of the Kydonians; linguistic proof of this theory he claims to have detected on the Hagia Triada tablets. Elsewhere Linear A inscriptions were composed in the Eteocretan language, which was of Hittite-Luvian origin. The correctness of the analysis is uncertain – as is another proposition that Linear A may be Semitic – for a case could be made out for the local development of writing in Crete, not least because the increasingly complex economic system based on the palaces needed written records. From Linear A inscriptions alone we cannot unravel the identity of the Minoans.

Linear B

At Knossos, but at no other site in Bronze Age Crete, Linear A was supplanted about 1450 BC by another script, which Evans first called Linear B. Although some of the Linear A signs also occurred in Linear B inscriptions, there were sufficient differences to suppose that the 3,000 tablets at Knossos represented another language. If this was the right deduction, which tongue did Linear B transcribe?

Right: One of the Linear B tablets found at the Palace of Nestor in Pylos. It was one of the first examples of linear script discovered in mainland Greece

In 1939 tablets like Knossian Linear B tablets were unearthed on the Peloponnese at Pylos. Of the initial 600 pieces the excavator, C. W. Blegen, noted:

Most of the signs on our tablets are seen to be identical with signs that occur on tablets of that class from Knossos, while the tablets themselves are strikingly similar to their Knossian counterparts, not only in composition and shape but in character as well . . . .

In some other respects, too, our deposit of tablets bears a remarkable resemblance to the one found in the Palace of Minos at Knossos, for in the southern corner of the room lying among tablets on the floor, were recovered remains of some half dozen badly corroded small hinges, perhaps the bronze fittings of a wooden box or chest in which documents were kept.

Pylos was the seat of King Nestor, the elder statesman of the Achaean Greeks. It was Nestor, 'the master of the courteous word, the clear-voiced orator', who tried to reconcile the enraged Achilles to Agamemnon, King of Mycenae, when they quarrelled on the plain of Troy. The *Iliad* says the ancient ruler 'had already seen two generations come to life, grow up, and die in sacred Pylos, and now he ruled a third'. It was clear that Blegen's find, thirty-nine years after Evans had encountered the first tablets in the ruins of Knossos, was proof for the use of Linear B script by a mainland administration. Between 1952 and 1954 excavations at Mycenae just outside the walls uncovered further tablets, thereby confirming the general use of Linear B script in the Peloponnese.

In 1939 Blegen was 'almost certain' that the language of the Pylos tablets was 'Minoan'. Like Evans, the amazing treasures recovered from the earth at Knossos persuaded Blegen that the cities of Pylos and Mycenae were merely provincial outposts of an island empire ruled over by a Cretan king. They were 'transmarine offshoots'. However, the discovery of tablets outside Crete led scholars to consider the possibility that Linear B was a Greek script. Various attempts were made to translate the inscriptions in Greek, but none of these was convincing.

One of the scholars who set to work was a young English

Opposite:
One of the giant *pithoi* found in the palace at Mallia

architect by the name of Michael Ventris. As a schoolboy his imagination had been fired by a lecture given in 1936 by Sir Arthur Evans on the occasion of the fiftieth anniversary of the British School of Archaeology at Athens. This enthusiastic amateur, whose decipherment was eventually to gain international approval, at first thought the language was Etruscan. An inscription in a tongue related to Etruscan was known from the island of Lemnos; the language of the pre-Greek Pelasgians, intermediate between Thracian and Hittite-Luvian, strongly recalled Etruscan, which may have derived from an archaic western Hittite dialect; and Greek tradition held that this Aegean people had once spread over most of the region. The balance of probabilities seemed to favour his diagnosis, which he maintained right up to the final stages of decipherment.

After the Second World War, Ventris decided to review progress and sent a detailed questionnaire to the dozen or so scholars working on Linear B. The replies offered no consensus but at least they encouraged the exchange of information. In particular the articles of Alice Kober, an American linguist, had a decisive influence on his thinking. She pointed out that even in an undeciphered state an inflexional language will have a visual declension. By systematic analysis of the signs used it might be possible to establish the syllabary. With the aid of three increasingly more complicated syllabic grids – tables showing which signs share the same consonant and which the same vowel – Ventris proceeded to analyse Linear B. When he looked at Cretan place-names such as Amnisos, Knossos, and Tylissos he found himself handling no fewer than thirty-one values of the syllabary containing some sixty-five signs of frequent occurrence. Once he began applying these values systematically to the inscriptions he noticed them exhibiting Greek inflexions. With the assistance of John Chadwick the conclusion was announced in a detailed article, 'Evidence for Greek dialect in the Mycenaean archives', which appeared in the 1953 issue of the *Journal of Hellenic Studies*. Dramatic support for the decipherment had come from a newly excavated tablet at Pylos. Immediately recognizable words on it included *ti-ri-po*, or tripod: Linear B was undoubtedly an archaic form of Greek.

The implication of Ventris' decipherment for Minoan history was equally startling. There had been a Mycenaean king of Knossos at the time when Nestor was ruling in Pylos. Homer was vindicated: from there an Achaean contingent had sailed to Troy. It began to look as if the effects of the Thera eruption around 1500 BC were to weaken the Minoan power to such an extent that Greeks from the mainland judged it safe, as much as fifty years later, to attack in strength and destroy all the centres of Minoan authority save one, Knossos, where a dynasty installed itself as the heir of Minos. Thus 1450 BC saw the collapse of Minoan civilization.

What do the Knossian tablets tell of conquered Crete? Not a

Opposite: Looking across the Central Courtyard at Mallia with the *kernos* in the foreground

Right: The 'grid' from Michael Ventris' 'Experimental Mycenaean Vocabulary' which set out his decipherment of Linear B for the first time. This was circulated privately in July 1952, the year before his conclusions were announced in the *Journal of Hellenic Studies*

Below: Part of a large Linear B tablet from Knossos

A / A_2	AI / E	I	O	U
JA	JE		JO	
F WA	WE	WI	WO	
G / K KA	KE / KE_2	KI	KO / KO_2	KU
CH				
T / TH TA	TE / PTE	TI	TO / TO_2	TU
D DA / DA_2	DE	DI	DO	
P / PH / B PA	PE	PI	PO	~~PTE~~
KW / GW / CHW	QE		QO	
L / R RA / RA_2	RE	RI	RO / RO_2	RU
M MA	ME	MI	MO	
N NA	NE	NI	NO	NU
S SA	SE	SI	SO	

great deal is the short answer. Even before Linear B was deciphered and the language identified it was evident to Evans from the script alone that:

> the great majority of the clay documents of Class B contained business records, such as accounts and inventories, and in nearly all cases are associated with numbers. The objects referred to by these lists are in most cases easily recognizable from the pictorial representations appended to the different entries . . . .
> We see here implements and weapons, chariots and their parts, and the cuirasses of royal charioteers, ingots, and the scales in which Minoan talents were weighed, precious vessels and others apparently containing various liquid products, granaries or storehouses on piles, and different kinds of cereals, the saffron flowers used for dies, several kinds of trees, domestic animals, including horses and swine, and crook signs which seem to indicate sheep or goats.

But the dedications to gods and goddesses are of considerable interest as they mention Zeus, Hera, Poseidon, Hermes, Athena, Artemis, and Eileithyia, whose sacred cave we noticed at Amnisos. Although Dionysos only crops up on two tablets at Pylos, this early evidence of the 'bull-horned god' has jolted accepted theories about his late arrival from Phrygia or Thrace. The labyrinth survives in Knossos as *du-pu-ri-to* on tablets concerned with honey but we cannot tell in what mysterious transformation the Lady of the Labyrinth was made to appear.

Above: The 'Tripod Tablet' from Pylos. Its inscription provided timely support for Ventris' decipherment

The Phaestos Disc

On 19 February 1910 an unusual photograph was printed in *The London Illustrated News*. It showed the enigmatic Phaestos Disc, the photograph having been sent in by Halbherr, the leader of the Italian archaeological mission on Crete. Readers were informed that the remarkable disc, according to its excavators, dates from 'the middle of the third millennium BC. The inscription contains about 250 hieroglyphic characters, representing arms, implements, ships, human figures, birds, helmeted heads, etc. The hieroglyphics do not belong to any known system, and there is no key at present to their meaning. They were evidently stamped on

Above:
The Phaestos Disc

Opposite: A drawing
of both sides of the disc
with the hieroglyphic
characters set
out underneath

wet clay, and this represents the first recorded attempt at printing in Europe.'

From the moment of this announcement the disc was the object of scholarly speculation, which generated an enormous literature and scores of unconvincing essays at decipherment. Evans fitted its picture-like signs into his own theory of the development of hieroglyphic writing and regarded the disc as an import from Asia Minor. In *The Aegean Civilization*, published during the 1920s, Gustave Glotz observed that of the signs represented 'a few only, such as did not allow of great differences, like the flower, the tree, or the fish, resemble the ancient hieroglyphs of the Cretans. There is nothing Minoan about the others, either in the type of the human figures or in the form of the objects; there are men in short tunics, fat women in double skirts, children in shifts, and houses like the Lycian pagodas . . . .The mere sight of such hieroglyphs, in addition to which there are manacles, the bow, the arrow, the ship, and the bird of prey, suggests the idea of an expedition undertaken

by one of the "peoples of the sea" mentioned by the Egyptian documents. Perhaps some tale of adventure could be read on the disc.'

The Philistines and the Lycians were advanced in turn as the authors of the Phaestos Disc, though some scholars objected that it was too fragile for transport over any distance. Notable but unconvincing translations were made into Greek and Basque in the 1930s. A school of thought, however, maintained that the disc was Cretan; evidence cited for its native origin was the existence of other spiral inscriptions of a religious or magical character on the island, and comparable signs incised on a bronze votive axe from a sacred cave at Arkalokhori as well as on an altar stone from Mallia. The difficulty of this interpretation remains the coexistence at Phaestos of an inscription of such under-developed syllabary and a proto-linear script, the antecedent of Linear A. The counterclaim, that the late survival of hieroglyphs in Crete, such as those of the Arkalokhori axe, the Mallia stone, and the Phaestos Disc, might be explained by their use as a sacred script long after linear characters had been employed for secular purposes, ignores the non-Minoan features of the script. The feather headdress, unknown on Crete, was worn by some of the peoples who in 1223 BC joined the sea raid on Egypt. In the Greek period this headdress was associated with the Carians of western Asia Minor. Yet these hardy sailors, according to Herodotus, provided the manpower for Minos' navy and they were armed with round shields. On the Phaestos disc the feather headdress and round shield occurs thirteen times. It seemed that the inscription might be composed in Carian, or more likely, it could have been a report on some aspect of Carian affairs. At least the hieroglyphs were provisionally placed within the family of Aegean and Hittite scripts.

Confirmation of the non-Greek tongue of the Minoans and the kinship of their language with that of the Hittites appeared to be given in the claim made by Vladimir Georgiev in 1976 that he had deciphered the Phaestos Disc. This Bulgarian linguist has put forward the case that the hieroglyphs record a Luvian dialect. The inhabitants of south-western Asia Minor, the region closest to Crete, spoke Luvian, a language related to Hittite, and the possible conclusion of Georgiev's contention is that Luvian-speaking people were ascendant on the island around 1700 BC, the age of the great palaces. Such an interpretation of Cretan history would fit the theory of early Luvian domination of large parts of the Aegean developed by Palmer, who, as we saw above, found some remarkable Luvian echoes in the Linear A inscriptions.

Georgiev is of the opinion that the Eteocretans and the Pelasgians, two pre-Greek peoples mentioned by Homer, had similar languages. He believes that 'this important linguistic feature of pre-Hellenic Crete must be taken into account in attempts to decipher the Phaestos Disc and Cretan inscriptions in the form of pictograms or Linear A'. He also points out that the hieroglyphs on the disc, with the limited number of signs, 'is perfectly suited to the Luvian language. Luvian possesses three vowels – a, i, and u; e scarcely ever appears – and twelve consonants. Almost all final consonants have become mute: it is almost entirely a language of open syllables, and the only consonant which can end an internal syllable is r. Consequently all Luvian words can be written with about forty syllabic signs.'

Of the Phaestos Disc, Georgiev further remarks in *Balkanskoto Yezikozanie*, its syllabary 'is the prototype, or nearly so, of pictographic Luvian writing. It contains many identical or similar signs, including the famous "tail". The difference is that the disc dates from the end of the seventeenth century BC, while the Luvian pictographic inscriptions range from the sixteenth to the eighth centuries BC. They come from different areas of southern Asia Minor or northern Syria, and include many local signs. Luvian pictographic writing is also influenced by Hittite cuneiform: it contains determinatives and ideograms that do not appear on the Phaestos Disc. Thus Luvian pictographic writing is simply a later development of the writing on this disc or of its prototype. On the other hand, these systems are akin to the Cretan hieroglyphic writing from which Linear A and B originated.'

The translation reveals a story of princely rivalry somewhere in Rhodes or Asia Minor. The disc is a brief record or report of the conflict prepared for the ruler of Phaestos by a certain Sanditimuwa, 'he who is strong through the god Sanda'. The text on side A reads:

When Iyara turned against Lilimuwa, when he attacked and failed, Iyaramuwa repelled him, chased away the favourite one and he himself crushed Lilimuwa. Tarhumuwa, however, decided concerning Iyara to rest. Tarhumuwa was at strife with Lilimuwa, but Tarhumuwa decided concerning Iyara to rest in the courtyard. He did violence to the frontier of Sandapi; Papimuwa escaped. Upparamuwa finds me angry about his own interest, but Runda does violence to him and repels him. Sarmassu, however, withdrew to the place of Iyaramuwa.

On side B the political situation becomes more complicated because of the intervention of a city state called Wilusa, probably Troy. Another famous city apparently involved in the intrigue is Apasa, later known as Ephesus. We read:

Sarma, however, considers and plans without check; he is encouraged. Wilusa pushes him, but I guard myself. Sarma, angry over Apasa, acts in his own interest. Wilusa pushes him on. Sarmassa freed himself, came, and pushed. Wilusa pushed him. For the humiliation of Iyarinu, he went to Ialusos, imposed a heavy tax, yielded, put out his eyes, and fled to Gazena. But Iyara was angry at the humiliation. Iyara garnered corn, ensured my well-being, and swears he could cause me no more troubles because it is in his own interest. Sanditimuwa.

The lack of a thorough understanding of the Luvian language would account for the lack of smoothness in the translation, but

Georgiev admits that he understands the side B less well. Some scholars are uncertain that he has got either side right, but at this moment in time his decipherment cannot be readily discounted. There is a strong possibility that Luvian was one of the languages spoken on Minoan Crete.

A multi-lingual civilization

Having indicated the surviving Greek traditions about ancient Crete and the surviving evidences of language use by the islanders, we must now turn again to the question posed at the very beginning of the chapter. Who were the Minoans? The first reaction of Evans certainly was justified. In Minoan civilization we find 'nothing Greek – nothing Roman'. Only at Knossos after the disaster of 1450 BC does archaeology reveal the presence of a new and warlike dynasty of Greek origin. Warrior graves and military scenes painted on the walls of the palace there fit the background of the Achaean warriors whom Homer described sailing to Troy. Evans himself had reported in *The Times* for 15 July 1907 traces of a *megaron*, situated in the western wing of the palace, but later he took the view that it was a temple built by the Dorians, not the Mycenaean Greeks. It would seem that this shrine was inserted at Knossos along with the remodelled Throne Room.

The Achaeans and the Dorians belong to the post-Minoan period. The builders of the great palaces, the navigators of the shores of the Mediterranean Sea, were people of non-Greek descent. Although the presence of a Greek dialect has been descried in the Linear A inscriptions from Hagia Triada by Georgiev, the linguistic arguments put forward to sustain this case lack assurance. His opinion of the Luvian nature of the Phaestos Disc is more persuasive. The Minoan world, recalling Homer's renowned list, consisted therefore of three peoples – the Eteocretans, the Kydonians, and the Pelasgians.

The language of the Linear A inscriptions we have recognized as that spoken by the Eteocretans. If Palmer is exact in his translation

A Linear A inscription on an altar from the Dictaean Cave. The last word may be Luvian for 'My Lady'

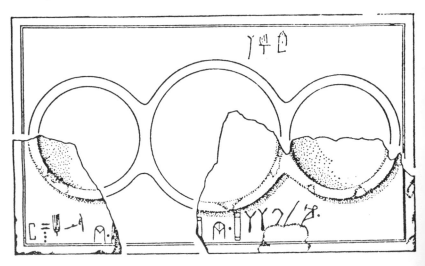

of the libation table dedication at Knossos, then the 'true Cretans' migrated from Asia Minor and their language was Luvian. Support for his hypothesis would come from a demonstration that certain place-names have Luvian stems. There is evidence that some Cretan place-names are Luvian. Tylissos, a town mentioned on the Linear B tablets, bears a strong resemblance to *tu-li-ya-as-si-is*, the adjectival form of the Luvian *tuliya*, 'an assembly'. Tylissos might have been originally called 'a place of assembly'. Other Minoan names also exhibit connections with Asia Minor. Minassos in Pisidia seems to be a formation from Minos, whilst the *labrys*, the double axe symbol of divinity, and perhaps kingship as well, may be connected with *labar-sa* found on Cappadocian tablets early in the second millennium BC. There was a Greek cult of Zeus Labraundos. In Hittite-Luvian *tapar* meant 'to rule', so that the related *t/labarnas* may have been the title of a ruler: at Knossos the king would have reigned in the labyrinth, the place of the double axe.

Like the later Greeks, the Luvians were invaders of Indo-European stock. Along with their nearer cousins, the Hittites, they had penetrated Asia Minor during the latter part of the third millennium BC. The Luvians were soon active in the west, their principal city of Beycesultan on the River Meander not being destroyed till 1750 BC, perhaps by the Hittite king Labarnas I, who 'made the seas his frontiers'. Luvians from Asia Minor may well have crossed to Crete prior to this event. Since the chief Minoan palace sites do not give any indication of a sudden change of activity but rather an intensification of previous development, it is to be supposed that such a migration would have occurred at the outset of the palatial period, before 1900 BC.

Of the other two non-Greek peoples recorded in the *Odyssey*, we know least about the Kydonians. They were the inhabitants of land around the city of Kydonia, modern Hania, but their language remains a mystery. The Pelasgians, on the contrary, we are aware from the histories of Herodotus and Thucydides to have been an Aegean folk. They had settled places like Thrace, Lemnos, possibly Attica, and Crete. Probably they had once spread over all the northern Aegean area and the greater part of the Greek mainland. Their language, as we have surmised above, was midway between Thracian and Hittite-Luvian. Herodotus informs us that the people of Attica were Pelasgians who had changed their speech to Greek.

The picture that emerges into focus, however indistinct, presents a composite population for Bronze Age Crete. At least three peoples inhabited the island before the arrival of the Greeks. The Minoan was a multi-lingual civilization. In ancient times such a situation would have been far from unique. There were no fewer than eight different languages in the archives of the Hittite capital.

4

Chronology and History

The Chronological Framework

The overwhelming impression on a visitor to the Archaeological Museum in Iraklion is the astonishingly high level of Minoan craftsmanship. Even in the pre-palatial period the Minoans were accomplished potters and workers in stone. Although the zenith of this remarkable artistic tradition was reached shortly before 1500 BC, the inventiveness of earlier Minoan potters ensured that many different shapes and styles already had been tried. At Knossos Evans used these various forms to create a framework for the chronology of Minoan history.

In 1904 Evans proposed, using pottery as a criterion, the division of Minoan civilization into three main periods: the Early Minoan period, represented by dark-surfaced and burnished wares found in the southern and eastern parts of Crete; the Middle Minoan period, when pottery with polychrome decoration on a dark ground became fashionable; and the Late Minoan period, characterized by elaborate vases and naturalist styles of decoration. The Early Minoan pottery is often called Sub-neolithic because the earliest phase is a transitional one, whilst Middle Minoan wares are known as Kamares after a sacred cave on Mount Ida where they were first noted in 1890. Each of the three main periods Evans then divided again into three, making nine phases in all.

Early Minoan I remained essentially Sub-neolithic, though new vase-shapes and thickened anti-splash rims were in evidence. Early Minoan II witnessed the arrival of many other new types of vase with light surfaces and decoration usually in red, but also in brown or black paint. A few dark-surfaced vases were also being decorated with creamy white paint. In Early Minoan III, a short phase, there was an increased use of white paint. The beginning of the Middle Minoan period was the point when decoration in two colours, a shade of red as well as white, appeared at Knossos. In Middle Minoan I two subsections were distinguished, A and B: the former characterized by polychrome vases often decorated with the spiral, a favourite Minoan design; the latter by clay vases that imitated the shapes and even the styles of decoration of metal ones.

82

Above left: A beaker jug in Kamares style; Middle Minoan IIA

Above right: A large jar showing Mycenaean influence; Late Minoan II or III

At this time the fast potter's wheel was introduced, but until the Late Minoan period the larger vessels were usually hand-made. Middle Minoan II represents the highest level for Kamares-style pottery, the washes being often a brilliant shiny black. Particularly fashionable too were the cups of metal-imitating egg-shell ware, products of the palace workshops of Knossos and Phaestos. A decline is apparent in Middle Minoan IIIA, another subdivided phase. Common in Middle Minoan IIIB, however, was a method of imitating the shimmering flutes of gold and silver vessels. Stripes were deliberately smudged by polishing the slipped surface of the vase while it was still wet. In Late Minoan IA and IB we reach naturalistic styles, with reeds and flowers soon giving place to extraordinary life-like octopuses, dolphins, starfish, and conches. The 'marine style' so magnificently set forth against a background of rock and seaweed was the culmination of the first attempts at naturalistic vase decoration made during Middle Minoan IIIA. Yet outside the palace workshops there was a lowering of standards, reflecting perhaps the difficulties confronting Minoan civilization immediately prior to the disaster of 1450 BC. Late Minoan II and III show Mycenaean Greek influence, the decoration becoming more formal and abstract.

Since Evans died in 1941 at the age of ninety, the Late Minoan III phase has been further subdivided into Late Minoan IIIA, B, and C. The pottery-based chronology is not accepted without criticism, and today stratigraphical research is being undertaken to check its validity. It has formed the chronological framework of Minoan history for a long time because of the immense reputation of its author. The shortcomings are threefold. In the first place, it was based on changes of fashion in pottery at Knossos. Yet even at this site, which must have been the pre-eminent one throughout the Bronze Age, there are considerable problems in deciding the period to which a particular vase belongs. The stratification of Knossos is not straightforward. Furthermore, the chronology lacks sufficient data from other sites, where of course the sequence of finds can be equally obscure. The centres of fine ceramic production were restricted to Knossos and Phaestos, so that elsewhere changes in pottery fashion could have followed quite separate provincial patterns. A final shortcoming was that Evans did not take account of the catastrophes that punctuated Minoan history.

An alternative chronological framework has been devised by Platon, the excavator of Zakro. He has based his system not on pottery styles but on architectural and cultural developments in the palaces. This offers four main periods, not three: Pre-palatial (2600–2000 BC), the period before the palace economies, corresponding with Early Minoan; First-palatial (2000–1700 BC), the period of the old palaces which ended through earthquake, and representing Middle Minoan I and II; Second palatial (1700–1400 BC), the period of the new palaces which replaced the first ones, that is Middle Minoan III and Late Minoan I and II; and Post-palatial (1400–1100 BC), the period after the destruction of the last surviving palace at Knossos, or Late Minoan III. But it should be noted that the date for the final conflagration there is still a matter of scholarly debate.

Dating systems

BC	Evans' scheme		Platon's scheme
6000 2600	Neolithic		Neolithic
2600 2200	Early Minoan I Early Minoan II Early Minoan III		Pre-palatial (2600–2000)
2100 1600	? ?	Middle Minoan Ia Middle Minoan Ib Middle Minoan IIa Middle Minoan IIb Middle Minoan IIIa Middle Minoan IIIb	First-palatial (2000–1700)
1600 1150	? ?	Late Minoan Ia Late Minoan Ib Late Minoan II Late Minoan IIIa Late Minoan IIIb	Second-palatial (1700–1400) Post-palatial (1400–1100)

The alternative chronological frameworks proposed by Evans and Platon

In order to determine the position of Minoan civilization in ancient history an absolute chronology had to be established for the Bronze Age. Evans relied largely on correlations with Egypt; pottery of Cretan manufacture had been discovered in Egypt, and Egyptian artefacts such as scarabs and stone vases in Crete. An alabaster lid inscribed with the name of Khyan, one of the most important Hyksos kings of Egypt, was recovered at Knossos in a deposit assigned by Evans to Middle Minoan IIIA. But the date of this find as well as other Egyptian objects has been challenged recently. Nor does the Carbon-14 method of dating greatly assist the Minoan archaeologist except in the lowest undisturbed levels of settlement. For the second millennium BC the dates available from tests are not very helpful. According to the radiocarbon method, the Minoan settlement on Thera was buried by around 1260 BC, whereas other evidence points to a date nearly 300 years earlier. At the moment therefore we lack precise dates for most of the key events in Minoan history.

Earliest settlers (c.6000 BC)

During the last Ice Age of the Pleistocene, when much of the water of the oceans and seas was locked up in the great ice sheets, the level of the Mediterranean was considerably reduced, so that the island of Kythera was joined to the Greek mainland, and the straits separating it from Crete would have been narrow. Across this stretch of water the hunters and food gatherers of the Old Stone Age could have swum or floated to the island. Yet at present archaeology puts the first traces of man on Crete in the New Stone Age, when there existed village settlements based on cereals, vegetables, goats, cattle, and pigs. The Neolithic village at Knossos, according to radiocarbon dating, started around 6000 BC. Excavation has detected ten successive building levels in the settlement mound, which is some 7 metres thick. The first houses were merely huts built of wood, but in level nine, where pottery is first found, the settlers used mud or mud brick and thatch for construction purposes. Later mud bricks rested on solid foundations as stone came into use. A typical Middle Neolithic house comprised a large rectangular room with one or two doors; inside were several storage bins, a fire-hole, and a bed platform. At Knossos the settlement was of agglomerate plan.

The earliest settlers seem to have stopped burying their dead inside their houses before they arrived in Crete. Only remains of a few children were discovered in the lowest levels of the Knossos mound. Caves were used for interments. The origin of these Neolithic people is unknown, though from current evidence of the distribution of early domesticated animals it would seem that features of their economy were imported from Asia Minor or West Asia.

The Bronze Age prior to the Palaces

About 2600 BC the Bronze Age started in Crete. Within a couple of centuries metallurgy was flourishing and handicrafts developed apace; pottery was decorated attractively – the Early Minoan I and II phases – and stone bowls carved from coloured rocks, while sealstones were minutely worked. At Vasiliki, a hilltop to the south of Gournia, we have a building that may be one of the forerunners of the later Minoan stone-built palaces. Ascribed to Early Minoan II, Vasiliki both recalls the agglomerate nature of the Late Neolithic settlement at Knossos and the complex of rooms seen in the later palaces. On the southern coast at Mirtos a similar Early Minoan II village has been located on the summit of a low hill. Less regular in plan than Vasiliki, partly because of the unevenness of the ground, Mirtos possessed stone foundations, mud-brick walls, sometimes covered with red plaster, rectangular rooms, and a primitive drainage system. From the site were recovered a copper knife, stone tools, vases, sealstones, seal impressions, and clay figurines. These two hilltop sites argue for the theory that the construction of the great palaces at Knossos and Phaestos were more the consequence of the increasing prosperity of Crete during the third millennium BC than foreign invasion. Colin Renfrew's *The Emergence of Civilization* is the masterly exposition of this case. Renfrew believes that contacts between Crete and both Asia Minor and Egypt from about 3000 BC were not critical factors in social development. On the contrary, he reckons the Minoan civilization was very much a European development, and that most of its features can be traced back, not to the older civilizations of West Asia, but to local antecedents and to processes at work in the Aegean over the preceding 1,000 years.

The question of invaders or refugees we prefer to leave open. As will be noticed in Chapter 3, in the field of philology, there is no clear-cut answer to the question of Minoan identity. It would not have been impossible for relatively small influxes of people to have taken place in the pre-palatial era, or after the destruction of the old palaces. Had the newcomers brought new techniques or new ideas with them, they could have assisted the striking advances in

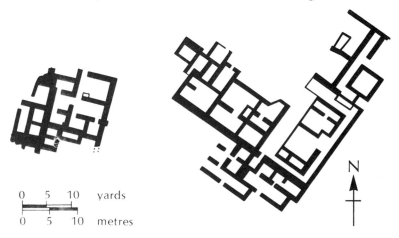

0 5 10   yards

0 5 10   metres

N

A comparison of the plans of a Late Neolithic house at Knossos (left) and the mansion at Vasiliki (right)

culture then happening. Around 1700 BC Palmer would introduce the Luvian dynasts of Knossos and Phaestos.

The early Minoans buried their dead in collective tombs, in caves, in rectangular ossuaries, in the round tombs of stone on the Mesara Plain, and in rock-cut chambers. In eastern Crete the dead seem to have been buried separately and their bones later transferred to the houses of the dead belonging to a family. The larger circular tombs on the Mesara could have served a clan, whilst the grouping of two or three tombs together suggests that an even wider kinship was recognized among the deceased. The inhabitants of the Cyclades appear to have adopted a similar custom. Although the Mesara tombs may have been the prototype of the Mycenaean *tholos* tomb, which however was deeply cut into a hillside, the attention paid to the living of a bygone era was not unduly elaborate. Burial did not involve animal sacrifice, and never the human sacrifice seen in the royal graves of early Egypt and Mesopotamia. Belief in the after-life is not easily gauged – the heavy stones at the doorway of some of the round tombs may have been intended to keep the dead from rising – but it should be remembered that the 'brother' of Minos, Rhadamanthys of Phaestos, was assigned by Greek legend to Elysium, not the grey underworld of Hades. Perhaps this enjoyable residence for the heroic dead like this Cretan lord was a survival from Minoan cosmology.

The Old Palaces (c. 2000–1700 BC)

Kingship and palaces. It is difficult to say how power came to be concentrated in the hands of a few rulers and what led to the founding of the first palaces. Certainly the material conditions were propitious for an urban revolution. We can trace the growing prosperity of the early Bronze Age economy in tomb architecture and funerary goods. Already, prior to the foundation of the first palaces around 2000 BC, there is evidence of an agricultural surplus capable of maintaining a highly-stratified society. Not only were Minoan farmers cultivating new plants such as the fig, the vine, the olive, and the date, but even more their industry had caused the authorities to make relatively elaborate arrangements for handling increased production. At Knossos an enormous underground chamber was constructed before the first palace there. Its purpose was most probably the storage of grain. In the design of Minoan palaces, and in the records kept in their archives, the importance of food storage can be discerned at once. The old and the new palaces were centres of a complicated redistribution system: all of them consigned extensive areas to the storage of foodstuffs. Each commodity received by a palace was sealed and noted, just as disbursements were meticulously inscribed on clay tablets. Mallia, whose ground plan for both the first and second palace was almost identical, had magazines specially designed to minimize waste of liquid and solid produce.

The old palaces have only been partially excavated because their ruins lie beneath those of the new palaces and are often inextricably mixed up with them. The old Palace of Minos built on top of the levelled settlement mound at Knossos was the model of palatial design, though Evans thought the building developed from a series of independent islands of buildings round a space which finally became the Central Court. Today we cannot be sure. Vasiliki indicates the initial stage of urban development, with a complex of buildings attached to an important person's residence. The old palace at Knossos, however, reserved a rectangular open space in the very centre of the building. It was the organizing nucleus of the layout: the palace faced on to this sunlit expanse of flagstones. Even the tiny palatial building in Gournia had a large courtyard close by. Yet the characteristic feature of Minoan palaces was the skilled use of limestone and gypsum blocks in their construction. There is nothing crude about the stonework. Minoan masons employed veneers of alabaster to conceal a wall of rough stone. They were able to achieve a sophisticated appearance by means of bronze saws and chisels, the practical relations of the double axe. In a very real sense the Minoan palace represents the zenith of the European Bronze Age. The Mycenaean citadel seems to belong to ruder civilization. In Crete there were no measures for defence, no great walls of 'Cyclopean' stone. The huge blocks of masonry, the wonder of the ancient and modern visitor to Tiryns, are monuments of an alien world.

The settlements surrounding the palaces consisted of densely-inhabited houses several storeys high. The Minoan town clustered about its palace, with streets radiating out from the entrances.

The great silos at Mallia which were probably used for storing agricultural produce

89

A ritual vessel painted
with stylized designs;
Late Minoan II

Population figures for the period 2000–1700 BC are little more than
intelligent guesses, but a cautious estimate would fill the palace
city of Knossos with not less than 20,000 people. Some of these
inhabitants have been excavated from *pithoi* graves and rock
covered ossuaries. One grave contained two razors of bronze,
bronze tweezers, and a mirror disc – a toilet kit for the after-life.

The construction of buildings so elaborate as the Minoan palace
required the services of a range of craftsmen: architect, stone-
mason, carpenter, plasterer, and painter. Built in them were workshops that in turn saw the skilful activities of other specialists:
potter, sculptor, lapidary or gem-cutter, glass-maker, faience-

maker, smith, armourer, tanner, and weaver. Besides these resident workers there were attendants expert in the cosmetic arts, bodily hygiene, cookery, and the serving of meals. In addition to guards, scribes, toreadors or acrobats, priests, and priestesses, the members of the court and the royal family had to be housed and fed. Indeed the palace, focal point for the agricultural organization of an area as well as for the redistribution of produce, acted as the vehicle for Minoan civilization. It called forth the creative originality of the ancient Cretans. When at last the palaces fell into ruin, the culture itself was shattered.

Best known of the arts and industry of the old palace period is Kamares-style pottery. The decoration is an elaboration of the white-on-black of Early Minoan III, but the advent of the potter's wheel made for polychrome ware of a fine fabric. Usual shapes were spouted jars, beak-spouted jugs, and handled cups. The Archaeological Museum in Iraklion contains a notable pedestal cup with applied sculptural flowers and links: it was unearthed at Phaestos.

The New Palaces (c. 1700–1450 BC)

A great earthquake on Thera in 1926 so impressed the excavator of Knossos that he would attribute the various catastrophes of Minoan civilization to the same cause. Evans was convinced that 'natural forces must largely account for the signs of ruin that here mark successive stages of the building'. His view was partly determined by his opinion that Mycenaean Greece was under the suzerainty of Minoan Crete. As we shall see below, the gigantic eruption of the Thera volcano did have a deleterious effect on the Minoan economy, but it was Mycenaean adventurers who turned this setback to their own advantage by means of fire and the sword. The disaster of 1450 BC was quite different from the natural destruction of 1700 BC.

Violent earthquakes demolished the old palaces round about 1700 BC, a date approximately fixed by comparisons with Egypt and West Asia. Owing to the extent of the disaster, the new palaces were, from the start, constructed to new plans. At Phaestos the ruins of the old palace were banked up and covered with a layer of broken tiles and concrete. The palaces whose ruined outlines can be explored today are these new palaces, though there are parts of the earlier structures left at Knossos and Phaestos. The old Mallia palace suffered the least damage and the reconstruction was consequently less dramatic.

During the period of rebuilding Minoan civilization acquired its definitive character. It was exemplified best in the delicacy of the new palace architecture. Glittering alabaster facades, delightful balconies and colonnades, expanses of sunlit courtyard juxtaposed with the coolness of subterranean passageways, airy ceremonial galleries above and still pillar crypts below, stairways, causeways,

The range of subjects
and the sophistication of
technique in the frescoes
discovered at Knossos
make these among the
finest examples of
Minoan art

Shown opposite: A
monkey and flowers,
part of a restored fresco
from the Palace of Minos;
a court dancer and the
dolphin fresco from
the Queen's room

Right: A detail of
partridges from a frieze
in the Caravanserai at
Knossos

Below: The Blue Bird
fresco from the palace

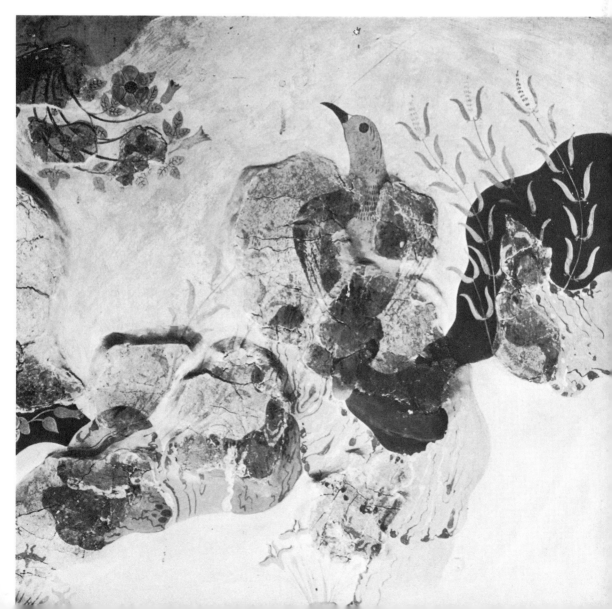

frescoed walls and patterned ceilings, and the discreet ubiquity of the downward-tapering column, the daily reminder of the chthonic power of the gods. Today the visitor to a palace site never feels oppressed, never overwhelmed. It must be partly owing to the peculiar charm of natural proportion which is in all Minoan things. In contrast with the temples and palaces of Egypt and Mesopotamia the scale of Minoan buildings is a distinctly human one. There is a sense of naturalness and spontaneity about what were once complex, labyrinthine constructions. The palaces do not seek to dominate or impress; they leave room for the human spirit to breathe freely. The ancient residents celebrated the abundance of life, whose tangible fruits overflowed into the passages of the magazines. Their worship would have joined them to the mysterious processes underlying the world. The intangible was glimpsed momentarily in the limbs and bodies of the court-yard performers, whether they stepped lightly through the intricate pattern of a sacred dance or leaped gracefully over the horns and back of a roaring bull. The Minoans knew their gods to their very finger-tips. They gave honour to them within the home as well as the palace. Everything they seemed to do was in terms of living.

In the arts the Minoan sensitivity was expressed in a feeling of grace, a love of movement, and a taste for elegance. As Henrietta Groenewegen-Frankfort succinctly remarked:

Cretan art ignored the terrifying distance between the human and the transcendent which may tempt man to seek a refuge in abstraction and to create a form for the significant remote from space and time; it equally ignored the glory and futility of single human acts, time-bound, space-bound. In Crete artists did not give substance to the world of the dead through an abstract of the world of the living, nor did they immortalize proud deeds or state a humble claim for divine attention in the temples of the gods. Here and here alone the human bid for timelessness was disregarded in the most complete acceptance of the grace of life the world has ever known.

Nowhere is the name of an artist to be found. Only the title of Minos – it seems not to have been a name – survives to designate the civilization. Daedalus, according to Greek mythology, was the first person to carve statues and construct buildings that were beautiful as well as inhabitable. He was the legendary epitome of the Minoan genius. But Daedalus likewise was not originally a personal name; it had connections with the labyrinth, since one of its meanings could have been 'a skilful thing'. An ancient tale says how Daedalus once solved a difficult problem connected with the spiral: the cunning artificer drew a thread through a snail shell.

Pottery decoration and mural painting were closely related in Later Minoan IA and IB. The motifs – lilies, tulips, reeds, grasses, and palms – can be discerned in the backgrounds of the new palace frescoes as well as on the sides of cups and jars. Human figures never appear in pottery decoration but the Minoan admiration of

energy and movement is evident on the 'marine-style' vessels manufactured by the palace workshop at Knossos. These wares, mostly of a ritual nature, were dispatched to every part of the island, and even to places overseas. Nearly every form of marine life is represented: argonauts, octopuses, dolphins, fish, and starfish are set against a background of corals, shells, sponges, and seaweed. The style disappeared on Crete about 1450 BC.

Other manufactures reached a high level of quality and design in the final years of the Minoan palaces. From 1550 to 1500 BC dates the so-called Harvester Vase of Hagia Triada, a masterpiece of stone-carving. This rhyton, the upper part of which only remains, portrays a sowing festival. A procession of farmworkers carrying on their shoulders hoes with willow-shoots attached to the ends is led by an older, long-haired man with a cloak and a stick. Midway in the group comes a singer brandishing a sacred rattle, who is followed by choir of three. The ivory-carver has also left us numerous exquisite examples of votive-offerings, including the gold and ivory snake goddess now kept in the Boston Museum of Fine Arts. Because the provenance of this miniature statue is unknown, there have been doubts concerning its authenticity, though contemporary opinion would ascribe it to sixteenth-century BC Knossos. Details of costume and feature – the thrown-back head and slightly arched body – make the Boston goddess the peer of the faience snake goddesses recovered there by Evans.

The Harvester Vase from Hagia Triada

95

Outstanding progress occurred too in fashioning bronze implements and utensils. The contents of the Tomb of the Tripod Hearth at Zapher Papoura, north of Knossos, bear witness to the advance in bronze and copperwork. Elaborate equipment for the service of wine and food was buried with the deceased: cups, basins, jugs, plates, ladles, a tripod cauldron, and a lamp. The tripod hearth itself is made of plaster. We can but guess at the grave goods of the Temple Tomb situated to the south of Knossos. What treasures of silver, gold, and precious stones must have been deposited in this royal tomb, the only one known to have contained the body of a Minoan ruler. The burial complex included a two-storeyed building with a porticoed court, a vestibule, a pillar crypt, and a sepulchral chamber cut into the rock: it recalls the legendary tomb of Minos in Sicily which was connected with a shrine of Aphrodite.

Thera and the Cretan disaster (c. 1500–1450 BC)

Some 90 kilometres north of Iraklion lies today the steep-sided island of Santorini, the remnants of ancient Thera. The island is the crater of a volcano, presently slumbering beneath the surface of the sea. Ships approach the harbour by sailing through one of the breaches in the crater-wall and anchor on a circle of water about 1,000 metres deep. Although the volcano was active on a small scale in 1939–41 and 1950–1, the last violent eruption occurred in 1926, when 2,000 buildings collapsed in forty-five seconds and convinced Evans that he had located the cause of Minoan decline. Previous eruptions of such intensity are recorded for the years 1650, 1707, and 1866. Scientific opinion on the Thera eruption of about 1500 BC is that it was the largest explosion in post-glacial time.

What caused the Cretan disaster? This question has not been satisfactorily answered. We shall review the possible events of the first half of the fifteenth century BC and put forward a theory that the collapse of Minoan civilization resulted from a combination of natural and human agency.

The fact of widespread destruction on Crete is plain. In the period Evans termed Late Minoan IB, probably close to 1450 BC, all the known Minoan sites in eastern, central, and southern parts of the island, excepting Knossos, were destroyed. The casualties were the palaces of Phaestos, Mallia, and Zakro; the towns of Palaikastro and Gournia, as well as those on the off-shore islands of Pseira and Mochlos; the great houses at Tylissos, Amnisos, Nirou Khani, and Sklavokampo. Sites were abandoned, or reoccupied partially, and the era of great material prosperity as well as notable achievement in arts and crafts came to an end. Only at Knossos does there seem to have been no dramatic break, no complete severance of palatial traditions.

The fact of the largest explosive eruption in human history is equally plain. Santorini is a huge volcano-crater and an enormous deposit of ash and rock. The activity of 1500 BC, or slightly later, must have had an effect on the economy and life of the Minoans. Crete was too near for its baleful influence not to have been felt. Yet how serious was this cataclysm?

The eruption of Krakatoa in 1883 offers a parallel. A much smaller *caldera*, or cauldron volcano, Krakatoa is situated between Sumatra and Java. For several months of 1883 the volcano was active. A series of explosions shook the region: the biggest one was heard in Australia over 3,000 kilometres away, and ranks as the loudest noise ever recorded on earth. Wind-borne ash fell at an even greater distance; tides rose on shores as remote as South Africa, Cape Horn, and India. Locally the Krakatoa eruption was more frightening in its impact. The sky was black with smoke and ash for two and a half days; walls and windows broke at 100 kilometres; hot ash and pumice rained down on crops and live-stock; and sea-floods on 27 August alone killed 36,380 people. The aftermath of the eruption would have been death from disease and starvation for the inhabitants of coastal areas had not tropical rains washed away the layer of ash settled everywhere. The lack of such downpours in Crete would have allowed the damage caused by ash-fall to be more lasting, if the island lay under the track of the wind-borne ash-cloud.

Panic. The immediate reaction to the Thera explosion must have been undiluted terror, as if the end of the world was nigh. The ancient Cretans could not have been unmoved by a natural phenomenon of such magnitude. What they thought of its mean-ing we do not know. Priests and priestesses would doubtless seek to reconcile the sudden violence with religious precepts – the anger of the gods or the unworthiness of men – but to kings and princes fell the task of salvaging the civilization. The extent of the damage we can only surmise, though surveys of the sea-bed indicate that a layer of ash was deposited on central, southern, and eastern Crete. New evidence from deep-sea sediment cores, published by an American research team in the January 1978 issue of *Nature*, establishes that ash settled to a thickness of up to 5cm. In Iceland it is documented that an ash-fall greater than 10cm resulted in the abandonment of farms, but a layer only half this thickness would have been a considerable inconvenience to the Minoans. Ancient agricultural techniques may have been less able to cope with ash than in more recent times. The American researchers conclude:

Our data suggests that the Minoan colonies on Rhodes and the south coast of Turkey may have suffered severe tephra-fall, whereas tephra-fall on Crete was probably insufficient in itself to cause a major decline of the Minoan civilization. We emphasize that our data does not, however, preclude a relationship between the eruption and the demise of the Minoan civilization. Present understanding of the direct effects (for example, tephra-fall) and indirect effects (for example, tsuamis, earth-quakes and meteorological phenomena) of very large explosions is very limited, as eruptions of this magnitude are yet to be chronicled.

So much for the ash-fall, a setback for agriculture though it may have been. We have now to consider the indirect effects, notably sea-flooding and earthquakes.

Of the coastal sites destroyed in 1450 BC none provides evidence of flood-waves. Gournia would have been overwhelmed by even a small flood because of its low position very close to the shore, but the archaeological evidence points to destruction by fire. On the other hand we know that earthquake was the destroyer of the old palaces. Tremors associated with the Thera eruption would account for the demolition of stone walls at Pseira, Amnisos, Mallia, and Zakro. However, the energy of a volcanic earthquake is seldom more than a very small fraction of that of a tectonic earthquake, which is produced by slidings and faults in the earth's crust. In this context, it is also difficult to explain the escape of Knossos, apparently well away from the seismic epicentre. The Palace of Minos was not only spared and modified but even more it became the seat of powerful princes who kept their records in the Mycenaean Greek of the Linear B tablets.

How then did Minoan civilization end? About 1500 BC Crete suffered the effects of the Thera eruption. Ash-fall covered the densely populated parts of the island, disrupting agricultural production and possibly reducing permanently the area under cultivation. At the same time some damage was sustained by buildings, though the intensity of the earthquake remains uncertain. Thera, Karpathos, Rhodes, and south-western Asia Minor certainly fared much worse. Damage outside Crete could have had repercussions on the Minoans, if there were close relations between these places and the island, but it would appear that this was less crucial than the weakening of the palace economies. The Minoans had built up an intricate civilization based on several palaces and mansions. Perhaps it was so delicately balanced that the Thera eruption was sufficient to inaugurate a decline. The fifty years prior to 1450 BC could have seen a dislocation of Minoan civilization – the perfect prelude to invasion. We suggest that this is what happened. The ultimate overthrow of the Minoans was the work of the Mycenaean Greeks, who took advantage of economic and social problems to conquer Crete.

The last palace at Knossos

Minoan civilization was in disequilibrium even before the arrival of the Mycenaeans. Its concentration at the palace nuclei made it very vulnerable to change, not to mention the sudden alteration of natural conditions brought about in 1500 BC. Without the palaces the civilization could not exist. And so it was that the destruction of the great centres extinguished the most genial and artistically original civilization in European history. The final blow was the Mycenaean conquest. Zakro, Sklavokampo, Mochlos, and Pseira were never reoccupied. At Gournia, Phaestos, and Mallia only parts of the town were rebuilt, while on the site of Hagia Triada alone a new palace arose, constructed according to Mycenaean notions. The invaders spared Knossos but not the buildings in the town outside the palace: the seat of Minos became the centre of power for the new dynasty.

The remodelled Throne Room was the main addition of the conquerors. Its fresco of guardian griffins, so proud and fierce in demeanour, anticipated the palace decoration at Pylos. The despatch of captive architects and artists to the Greek mainland after 1450 BC could have been responsible for the rapid spread of Minoan taste. A gradual process of 'minoanization' had been already at work for centuries, a cultural export to the increasingly wealthy but less refined mainland kings, yet the total Mycenaean domination of the Aegean in terms of trade and power must have led to a shift of activity away from Crete. It was the final stage of the Mycenaean takeover of Minoan culture and religion.

The rulers of the last palace of Knossos were nonetheless un-Minoan. The weapons deposited in their rock-cut tombs suggest a degree of militarism hitherto unknown on Crete. This warlike impression is strengthened by the appearance of chariots on frescoes and the military equipment listed on the Linear B tablets. The Mycenaean dynasts ran the island for their own personal benefit.

About 1375 BC Knossos, according to Evans, was burnt to the ground, the flames fanned by a wind blowing from the south. The incendiaries are unknown. They may have been the Minoans in revolt against their Mycenaean masters. Or perhaps the Mycenaean warrior chiefs, so prone to squabbling among themselves, destroyed the palace through a personal feud. The disastrous expedition to Sicily, recorded in Greek legend, could have taken place at this time and undermined the foreign lords of Knossos. We cannot tell. Evans favoured an earthquake or a series of quakes. An intriguing alternative is offered by Palmer. From philological and archaeological evidence he argues that Knossos was continuously occupied by Mycenaean Greeks till the very end of the Bronze Age (c. 1150 BC). Such a theory would make the Dorian Greeks, armed with sharp iron swords, the destroyers of the Palace of Minos.

Amnisos, the port of Knossos. The remains of Minoan houses are visible in the foreground, while in the far distance lies the island of Dia, where Ariadne died

5

Minos, King of the Sea

For Homer, Minos was a son of Zeus by the daughter of Phoenix, the eponym of Phoenicia. She, in Greek mythology, is called Europa. The daughter of the king of Tyre, Europa used the cosmetics of the great goddess Hera in order to entice Zeus. Hiding among cattle disguised as a bull, he behaved so gently that she climbed on his back. Immediately Zeus galloped to the shore, and swam across the sea to Crete where he carried her to his birthplace, the Dictean Cave. There Europa bore to the god three sons, Minos, Rhadamanthys, and Sarpedon. That Homer and the mythological tradition name as her father a West Asian prince, a Phoenician, must mean at least that the ruler of the ancient Cretans, the legendary Minos, was known to the Greeks as a non-Greek, if not actually an Asian, king. In all probability this lineage represents a dim recollection of the unusualness, the unique flowering of Minoan civilization. Minos' palace was like nothing else in the Aegean, while Crete also boasted smaller palaces of considerable splendour. There is some evidence for Phoenician activity in the region: Herodotus states that the famous shrine of Aphrodite on the island of Kythera was founded by Phoenicians after the model of that goddess' temple at Ashkalon. The Greek historian adds that Kadmos, the brother of Europa, searched the islands for her, and left behind on Thera 'either because the land was pleasant, or for some other reason . . . among other Phoenicians, his kinsman Membliaros'. Whether only Minos, or one of the kings of Knossos who may have borne the title Minos, was a descendant of Phoenician seafarers remains an unsolved mystery. The idea of a powerful foreign lord of the waters, a commander of ships that swiftly took men and merchandise to and from Amnisos, the busy port serving his palace, was the part of Minoan civilization remembered by the Greeks in their traditions.

The Cretan supremacy

The half millennium between 2000 and 1500 BC was the time when Minoan vessels roamed unchallenged on the Aegean Sea. The total absence of fortifications about ancient Cretan settlements would

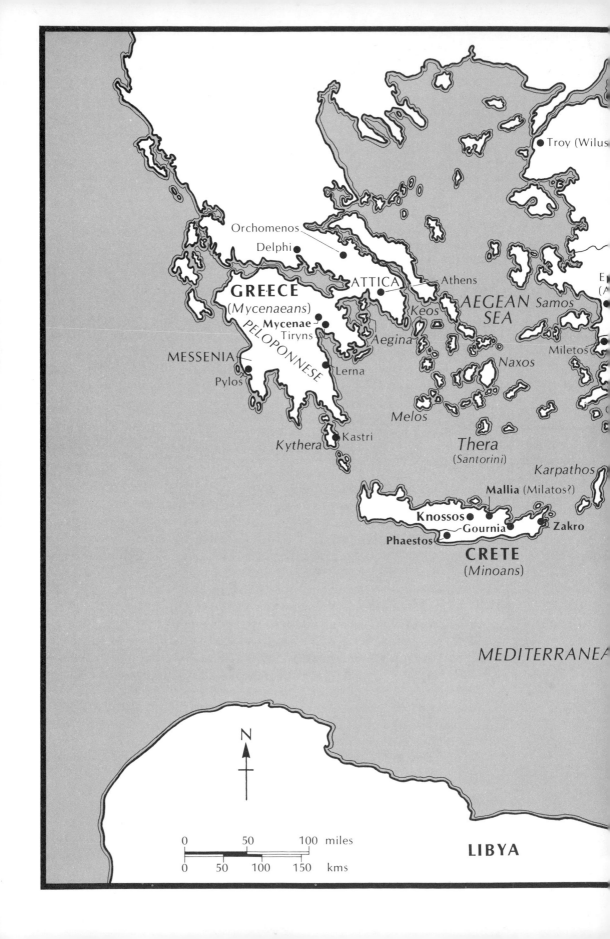

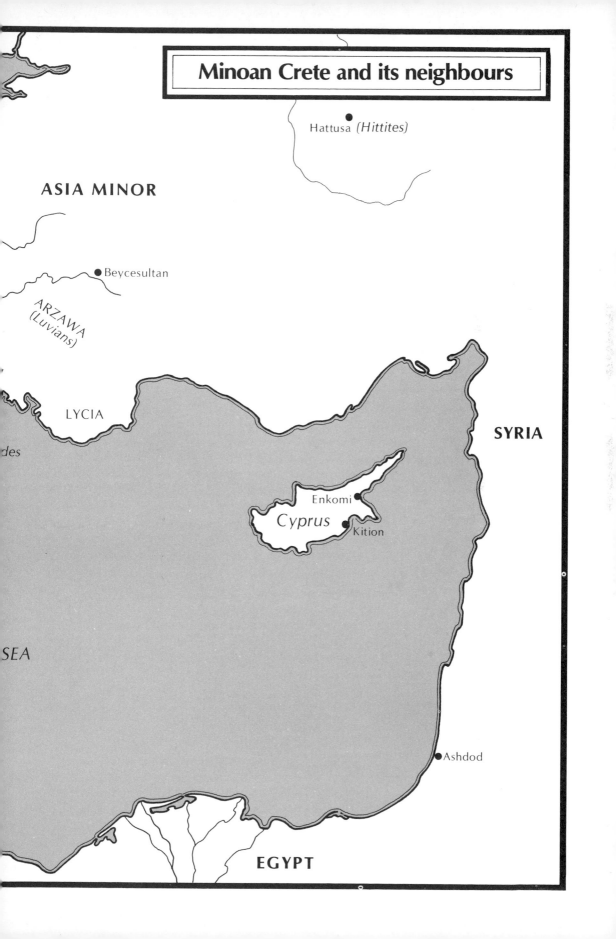

Minoan Crete and its neighbours

Hattusa *(Hittites)*

ASIA MINOR

●Beycesultan

ARZAWA
(Luvians)

LYCIA

SYRIA

des

Enkomi●

Cyprus
●
Kition

SEA

●Ashdod

EGYPT

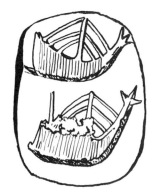

Seals showing Minoan ships; these may be compared with the vessels shown on the Thera frescoes on pages 114–5

vouch for this supremacy, even without reference to the archaeological traces of commercial contact with surrounding lands. The power of Minos was accepted as a fact by Greek historians and many local legends support the reputation of the Cretan navy. People said that Minos came to Keos with his fleet; Samos was believed to have been settled by Minoans; Sarpedon is reported to have founded Asiatic Miletos at the same time; while the Termilians of Lycia claimed that their ancestors had originated in Crete. On the Greek mainland the influence of the Minoans was also felt, when Minos attacked Nisaia in the Megarid, Rhadamanthys held Boeotia, and the Athenians were obliged to pay an annual tribute of seven maidens and seven youths to feed the Minotaur. The many places named Minoa were patent reminders of the former authority of the kings of Knossos.

From the archaeological testimony Evans proposed Minoan conquest overseas. Although the theory of dominance in the Aegean does accord with Greek traditions, there are practically no signs of a direct relation between Crete and mainland Greece prior to 1500 BC. Like the later Greeks, the Minoans planted colonies abroad, traces of which are found on Thera, Melos, Kythera, Rhodes, and Keos, but it seems improbable that Minos sought to subdue neighbouring peoples. On the contrary, the spread of Minoan cultural influence might have been connected with the rise of the Mycenaeans. Their increasing wealth would have allowed the purchase of Cretan exports and skills.

The coasts of Crete were protected by both sea and ships. The main function of the Minoan fleet was the elimination of pirates, so that the seaways remained safe for commerce. From earliest times privateering and brigandage had been an alternative to business. When conditions were unstable, and trading vessels could not sail between ports because of the activities of pirates, there occurred a recession that lasted for decades rather than years. The economic system that generated the Cretan navy – the palace regulation of agriculture and industry – was the chief beneficiary of its effectiveness in terms of international trade. From Knossos and the other centres of production went out manufactured articles such as vases and jewellery as well as raw materials like wool and timber. The Minoans grew rich on trade, not battles.

The little that we know about the ships of the Minoan navy and merchant marine came until recently from tiny engravings on seals. The discovery of naval scenes in frescoes excavated on Thera has added considerably to our still limited knowledge. Favoured by ancient Cretan shipwrights were rounded hulls, not the angular-ended types common in the Cyclades. Illustrations dating from about 1500 BC reveal a vessel with a slender, rounded hull, and an unornamented prow and stern; it was propelled by oars as well as a single broad sail. Large merchant vessels were decked and those carrying passengers had a shelter upon the deck too.

The Minoan warship may have been fitted with a ram, like

Greek ships, but no pictorial evidence has been discovered so far which indicates that this was a method of attack used by Minos' admirals. According to Herodotus, the sailors themselves were the natives of Caria, then called Leleges.

The growth of Mycenaean power

Evidence of a change in the Aegean balance of power exists in Egyptian tombs. Foreigners, who appear to be Cretans by their attire and the gifts they are presenting to the pharaoh, are depicted in the tombs of high officials at Thebes. On the walls of the tomb of Rekhmire, vizier under Thotmes III (1504–1450 BC), these visitors are labelled 'men of Keftiu and the Islands'. They were intended to be Minoans from Crete, and their colonists or allies from other Aegean islands. All of them are wearing decorated kilts reminiscent of those in the fresco along the Corridor of the Procession at Knossos. But when the paintings of Rekhmire's tomb were being cleaned several years ago it was discovered that the figures of the 'men of Keftiu and the Islands' had been altered. Originally they were painted with cod-pieces of the kind associated with the short, stiff kilt, upturned at the back.

The change in fashion must have been important enough in the eyes of the Egyptian artist to merit record. None of the other foreigners shown bringing gifts or tribute were repainted. What does the alteration of dress mean? Most likely is the theory that it represents two separate embassies from the Aegean to Egypt. The first embassy, clad in the old Cretan kilt, might have arrived from Knossos at the behest of the Minoan ruler, whereas the second one, late in the reign of Thotmes III and after the disaster of about 1450 BC, was probably sent by the Mycenaean overlord, who would have been anxious to gain recognition and inherit Minoan trading rights. Although the long kilt of the Mycenaean envoys was

The Rekhmire tomb painting showing Minoans bearing ingots and rhytons

already worn in Crete before this time, and may have even developed there, it seems to have been readily adopted by the inhabitants of the mainland.

Knossos survived the Mycenaean Greek invasion around 1450 BC because it provided a suitable base for military dominance and economic exploitation. The selective destruction of the conquerors underlines this dual concern. The sacking of Knossos in 1375 BC, if indeed such was the date at which the last palace was destroyed, could be explained in terms of continued rivalry between the Greek mainland and Crete. Another expedition from Mycenae and the other centres of power might have had the avowed object of breaking the economic influence of Crete, which would have recovered to a considerable extent under foreign dynasts. For a time after 1450 BC Cretan exports to West Asia and Egypt, to judge from the pottery found there, persisted alongside Mycenaean ones, but in the early fourteenth century Cretan goods stopped completely and mainland wares flooded the market. The second attack on Knossos would have been a dress-rehearsal for the Trojan War. The *Iliad* seeks to justify the 'sacker of cities', giving a sentimental reason for an economic war, yet it was the very arrogance and belligerence of the Mycenaean Greeks that cost them the riches of international commerce. Menelaus was actually raiding Egypt at the time of Helen's abduction. The consequence for the Aegean of differences with the pharaohs was the cessation of trade with Egypt for a couple of centuries. To compensate for this loss the Greeks were obliged to turn to the north and grasp at the wealth of Troy.

The beginnings of the warlike Mycenaeans are discernible in the Peloponnese and central Greece after 2000 BC. Intruders established themselves in strongholds and by mixing with the indigenous population created the earliest Greek civilization, named Mycenaean after its foremost city. Much was owed to the submerged culture as well as to the influence of Crete. Some of the warrior-chiefs may have been even descendants of settlers from Asia Minor, the Luvians who Palmer believes overran the Greek mainland shortly before this time. In the south-western corner of the Peloponnese Minoan influence seems to have been strong from the sixteenth century BC. *Tholos* tombs are numerous in the vicinity of Pylos and appear to have been built there earlier than in any other part of the mainland. Some of them stood entirely above the ground like the circular tombs of the Mesara, and the dependence on Cretan technique indicates the impact that this island civilization had on the Mycenaeans. But not all features of Mycenaean civilization should be attributed to a Minoan model. Excavation at Lerna in the Argolid has revealed a settlement fortified by a wall with bastions. Called the House of Tiles, after the roofing material found there, this building is comparable and contemporary with the Minoan country house at Vasiliki. There are also signs in other sites dating from the middle of the third millennium BC that a high level of craftsmanship existed prior to the arrival of Greeks, or any other non-Aegean people.

Minoan conquest or settlement outside the Aegean is doubtful. The Mycenaeans on the mainland were always contentious and they adopted an architecture already distinguished by its fortifications. Tiryns was the culmination of a process of military specialization that had begun in Neolithic times. The refinements of civilized living were borrowed from Crete but the 'minoanization' of Mycenaean Greece was in some ways rather superficial. The ancient Cretan legacy of Greek civilization was not inherited until after the Mycenaean occupation of Knossos. Then only could mainland princes offer attractive work to unemployed Cretan palace staff. The relationship between Crete and mainland Greece prior to the disasters of the fifteenth century BC was mutual respect and non-interference. What brought about the change of circumstances so carefully recorded in the Rekhmire mural was the aftermath of the Thera eruption. Equally aware of the new balance of power in the Aegean were the Hittites. A letter survives from the Hittite king to his 'brother' the king of Ahhiyawa, or the Achaeans. The subject of the letter is Miletos, where the king of Ahhiyawa kept an agent by the name of Atpas, to represent his interests. The Minoan foundation of the colony goes entirely unmentioned.

Minos, Sarpedon, and Rhadamanthys

The Minos who quarrelled with Sarpedon was one of the Minoan rulers of Knossos. There were doubtless several Cretan kings called Minos: three prominent in Greek tradition were Minos the contemporary of Sarpedon, Minos the husband of Pasiphae, and Minos the victim of Kokalos, the king of Kamikos in Sicily. The relationship of the first two is sufficiently close in legend to hint that we have here an accretion of stories about one or two generations of the early lords of Knossos. The Minos who died in a Sicilian bath we propose in the next section to have been a Mycenaean Greek.

Sarpedon, in Greek mythology, assisted Troy against the Achaean host. He was supposed to have led the Lycian contingent of Priam's allies. In the *Iliad* he took a prominent part in the fighting, staged a daring assault on the Greek camp, and was of great aid to the hard pressed Trojans until he felt the keen point of Patroclus' spear. Sarpedon's heroic death on the plain before the walls of Troy and his disagreement with a Minos then long dead was explained by supposing that he lived for three generations. Even this span of time would have been inadequate to make Sarpedon the brother of Minos and Sarpedon the cult-hero of Lycia the same historical person. The Cretan connection, it is thought, recalls an historical relationship between the Minoans and the Lycians.

Involved in a quarrel with Minos, Sarpedon fled to Asia Minor where he founded Miletos. The excavations of the site suggest that the colony was established in Middle Minoan IIIB, not later than 1600 BC. The expulsion of a 'brother' king from Cretan Milatos, or Mallia, could be seen as part of the creation of Knossian authority. Minos needed to assert his kingship of the island before he was recognized as king of the sea. The implication of the legend is that once Sarpedon was of equal rank with the king of Knossos.

The other brother of Minos was called Rhadamanthys, demonstratively a non-Greek name. With this 'brother' king also Minos disputed the rule of Crete. According to an ancient Cretan genealogy Rhadamanthys was the son of Phaestos and the father of Gortys, a city that in Roman times was to become the capital of the province of Crete and Cyrene. These associations imply that Rhadamanthys was once the ruler of the Mesara, where Phaestos was the chief city. During the Middle Minoan period Phaestos was clearly the centre of a very prosperous kingdom in southern Crete. By the time of the Linear B tablets at Knossos, however, Phaestos was dependent upon Knossos, often being listed on the palace records. It is quite possible that the overlordship of Knossos was accepted well before the coming of the Mycenaeans in 1450 BC.

Minos, Sarpedon, and Rhadamanthys were sons of Europa, who was brought from Phoenicia by Zeus. The Greeks remembered the oriental heritage of the Minoan kings as well as the Minoan preoccupation with bulls. Not only was Europa fascinated by a bull incarnation of a god but even more it was her eldest son Minos who prayed to Poseidon to send a bull from the sea for him to sacrifice. The sea-god obliged, thus confirming his right to rule, but the beast was so handsome that Minos would not kill it. Enraged by this sacrilege and slight, Poseidon caused Pasiphae, Minos' queen, to fall in love with it. By the help of Daedalus, who constructed a hollow wooden cow, which he upholstered with cow's hide, Pasiphae deceived the bull, and attained her pleasure; consequently, she bore a creature half-man, half-bull. It was the Minotaur, 'Minos' bull, which lived in the labyrinth. The drift of the legend, especially in Attic traditions, now turns sombre and threatening. Minos is 'evil-minded' and the cruel tribute of young people to feed the Minotaur begins. The intervention of Theseus and the slaying of the devouring beast – which is not in the mainstream of Greek mythology – probably has behind it an historical contest between ancient Attica and Crete. The murder of Androgeos, son of Minos, at the order of the Athenian king might echo an actual clash of arms on the Attic shore: legend says that Androgeos was ambushed leaving the All-Athenian Games, where he had won every contest.

Rhadamanthys, on the other hand, escaped death altogether. He was translated to the Elysian Fields, a paradise which Homer placed in the far west, on the banks of the encircling river Oceanus. The uncle of Rhadamanthys, Kadmos, ended also in Elysium, though as a serpent. Having searched in vain for his sister Europa, he was ordered by the Delphic Oracle to build a city in Boeotia, a foundation later known as Thebes. The Greeks credited Kadmos with the introduction into Europe from Phoenicia of an alphabet of sixteen letters. Rhadamanthys, too, was wise and just, like Minos consulting every nine years with Zeus. Both Minoan kings became judges of the dead, but Minos failed to reach the perfect peace of the pre-Greek abode of Elysium. Rhadamanthys was credited with bringing a tough cane into Boeotia: this Cretan plant was cut for javelins and flutes. The descendants of Phoenix were thus often cultural founder-heroes for the Greeks, and it is tempting to see in this legendary fame a reflection of the former glories of Minoan civilization.

Minos and Sicily

The Theseus legend is sometimes used to explain the overthrow of the Cretan supremacy, but the story does not attribute to Theseus the destruction of Knossos. The killing of the Minotaur removed from Athens the human tribute on which the creature was kept; but even in the most favourable Attic versions the hero does not destroy the Palace of Minos. The legend is best read as a memory of the assertion of Athenian independence. We must look elsewhere for an explanation of the final eclipse of Cretan naval power.

The tradition of Minos' death at Kamikos may offer a reason for the vulnerability of Crete after 1450 BC. The fullest account of the event occurs in the historical writings of Diodorus Siculus. As the fateful expedition to Sicily was launched to find the fugitive Daedalus, we should start by considering this enigmatic architect and engineer. His name contains the notion of things cunningly wrought. The Greeks regarded Daedalus as the first artist: with his subtle mind and skilful hands he had transformed craftsmanship into art. His works, Plato thought, were tinged with divinity. It was said that his statues were so lifelike that they had to be chained to prevent them from running away. That in later times Daedalus, though given an Athenian birth, was mostly associated with Minos, a ruler of Knossos, must mean at least that his greatest inventions and constructions were supposed to have been achieved on Crete. It is probable that Daedalus' origin was a later accretion to the basic legend, and that Crete was in fact his native country.

Daedalus had arrived in Knossos as a refugee. He had been expelled from Attica for the murder of his nephew, Talos, who rivalled him in skill and ingenuity. Minos warmly welcomed Daedalus and for some time he lived in high favour and peace. A work for his new patron was the famous labyrinth. One day, however, Minos, learning that Daedalus had helped Pasiphae to couple with Poseidon's bull, imprisoned him in the labyrinth, together with his son Icarus. Even with the help of Pasiphae, the two prisoners could not escape from the island, so absolute was

Minos' control of the sea. Daedalus rose to the occasion and invented serviceable wings for himself and his son. Whilst the king of Knossos was impotent once they had taken flight above the island and the sea, Daedalus was placed in exactly the same position as regards Icarus, whose impetuosity led him to fly so high that the wax holding together the feathers of his wings melted. Daedalus buried Icarus on a near-by island and then sped on to Sicily.

An alternative story is that Daedalus invented sails, not wings, as a means of outstripping Minos' galleys; and that Icarus, steering carelessly, was drowned when their boat capsized. Whatever the method of flight employed, its superiority over Minos' transport would have been reason enough for that monarch to give chase. No Bronze Age king could afford the technical abilities of such a skilled craftsman to be at the disposal of a rival. Daedalus was as capable of building warships and strongholds as he was palaces and shrines. Moreover, the Mycenaean dynasts of Knossos needed an architect to remodel their palace late in the fifteenth century BC. To a great extent the prestige of a ruler depended on the possession of a palace more imposing than his brother monarchs'. Daedalus, we suggest, tired of working for Greek usurpers, and disappeared from Crete before his work was complete.

At this point we shall let Diodorus Siculus take up the story:

Meanwhile, Minos had raised a great fleet, and set out in search of Daedalus. He brought with him a shell, and wherever he went promised to reward anyone who could pass a string through it – a problem which no one but Daedalus would be able to solve. Landing in Sicily, Minos offered the shell to Kokalos, the king of Kamikos, who undertook to have it threaded. This Daedalus did . . . and, when Kokalos claimed the reward, Minos demanded the architect's surrender. But the daughters of Kokalos were unwilling to lose Daedalus, who made them beautiful toys, and with his help they plotted Minos' death. Daedalus led a pipe through the roof of the bath, down which they poured boiling water, or oil, upon Minos, while he was washing himself.

Kokalos handed over the corpse to the Cretans, who buried the dead king 'with great pomp'. Minos' tomb occupied the centre of Aphrodite's temple at Kamikos, and there his bones remained till in the fifth century BC they were returned to Crete by Theron, the tyrant of Akragas.

The description of the tomb corresponds so closely to the arrangement of the Temple Tomb south of Knossos that a Minoan-Mycenaean royal tomb had certainly been known in Sicily. Excavations of burial chambers around Akragas indicate the influence of the *tholos* tomb. It would appear, therefore, that the Sicilian tradition recorded by Diodorus and the Cretan tradition of Minos' death in Sicily recorded by Herodotus had an historical basis.

The Sicilian expedition was a disaster, a forerunner of the Athenian one at Syracuse in 413 BC. 'After the death of Minos',

Herodotus noted, 'the Cretans fell into total disorder, because their main fleet was burned by the Sicilians. Of the crews who were forced to remain overseas, some built the city of Minoa, near to the shore where they had landed; others settled at Hyria and places inland.' The Cretan tradition obviously refers to an armada that sailed to avenge the death of the king of Knossos. It suffered defeat and shipwreck, being the cause of the end of Cretan naval power. The vulnerability of the island afterwards was legendary. If the civilization built up by the Minoans had not already sustained irreversible damage when the Mycenaean Greeks took over control of Crete in 1450 BC, shortly after the Thera eruption, then the loss of men and resources in the Sicilian venture would have been sufficient to destroy it. As it happened, the island 'of ninety cities' became the prey of adventurers and rebel bands. The destruction of 1450 BC must have seemed almost moderate in comparison. The final conflagration at Knossos, if 1375 BC is accepted as the correct date, would fit into an historical sequence of events that left its pugnacious occupants considerably weakened. There is some evidence of a fall in population about this time in central and southern Crete. It conforms, furthermore, with the statement of Herodotus that the people living at the eastern end and the western end of the island did not participate in the expedition to Sicily. The descendants of the Kydonians were certain that western Crete had contributed no ships.

Bronze ingots in the shape of oxhides found at Hagia Triada. They have a uniform weight of 29 kilos

International trade

Ancient Crete occupied a key position in Aegean trade. Geography had not only provided convenient seaways to the Greek mainland and the Cyclades in the north; and to Sicily and Italy in the west: it had, moreover, given the Minoans an island endowed with natural resources that generated an economic system capable of maintaining a high level of internal and external trade. While much of this commercial activity may have been controlled by the palaces, a class of private merchants no doubt existed as in East Asia and Egypt at the time.

Trade in the pre-palatial era had advanced slowly. Internally, the increased agricultural surplus permitted a degree of specialization that gave rise to local centres of handicraft production, which later were concentrated in the palace workshops. Although for their basic needs the Minoans were self-supporting, a number of commodities like tin and precious stones were lacking in Crete and this shortage encouraged contact with the other islands of the Aegean as well as Cyprus and Syria. During the period of the palaces, in the first half of the second millennium BC, there was a notable expansion of international trade, called into being by the growth and sophistication of the Cretan economy and protected by the efficiency of Minos' galleys. Crete was the dominant region in the Aegean culturally and economically, if not politically. The same was true in the Late Minoan I and II periods, though Mycenaean trading activity becomes more evident in the archaeological record. After about 1375 BC the Mycenaean Greeks assume first place both in the Aegean and beyond. Trade with Syria, however, may have developed as a Cypriot monopoly, since the first Mycenaean enclave in Cyprus is thought to date from only 1200 BC. Great quantities of Mycenaean pottery are found all over the area, but the even larger amounts of Cypriot pottery accompanying them suggests that trade was challenged through the flourishing ports of Enkomi and Kition. A sharp decline in Aegean trade generally takes place around 1200 BC.

Minoan ports were usually situated on small promontories offering a harbour on either side according to the direction of the wind. Mochlos, now an island, may have been a peninsula in the Bronze Age. From these ports sailed the ships of the Minoan merchant marine. How reliable these vessels were can be gauged from the commission issued by Thotmes III in 1467 BC. When the pharaoh wanted to ensure the safe arrival of a consignment of cedar-wood from Phoenicia, he chose to employ the 'men of Keftiu'. From the forests of Crete the trusty Minoans must have exported timber to Egypt as well. In exchange for wood and olive oil – products in short supply in Egypt – the sailors would have been pleased to accept textiles, then rated next after gold in value as a commodity of exchange.

The Minoans did not have to bring food or building materials from abroad: they possessed wood, stone, and land enough at home. The wealth and splendour of the palaces could only be supported through the production of large surpluses and the employment of a large workforce. The Linear B tablets bear witness to both. The reserves of olive oil certainly allowed for export, but there is little reason to presume that grain was ever in permanent surplus. A leading export product must have been woollen cloth, given the palace interest in sheep-raising and textile manufacture. There is abundant evidence too for a considerable trade in painted pottery. From 2000 BC onwards Minoan wares reached the Aegean, Cyprus, Syria, and Egypt. The large quantities of finds at

Opposite above:
The Spring Fresco discovered during excavations on Thera

Opposite below:
Another fresco showing the Minoan's mastery of natural subjects; a monkey and flowers discovered at Knossos

Overleaf: The Naval Campaign fresco from Thera, which gives unique evidence of Minoan ships and architecture

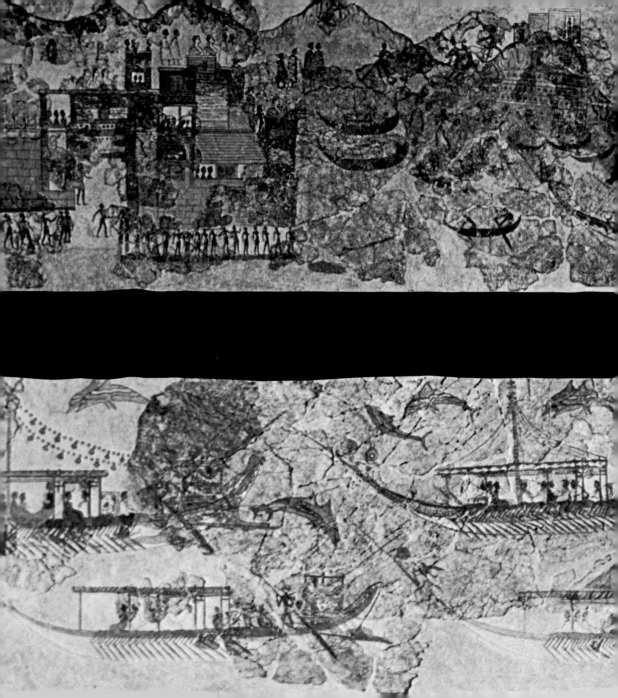

Above: A detail of the Spring Fresco found on Thera

Opposite: The Fisherman from another Thera fresco

Ubiquitous bronze; examples of the metal implements and tools upon which Minoan civilization was based

Trianda on Rhodes, for instance, has led to the suggestion of direct influence in the form of a Minoan colony. Other luxury items sent overseas included stone jars, clay lamps, and bronze daggers. When the Minoans exported goods, they treated them with care. Oil-pitchers were closed with a clay seal, one of which Evans interpreted in his study of the hieroglyphic script. The hundreds of sealings recovered from Cretan sites show a strict regulation of commerce, but our knowledge of the standard weights and measures used by the Minoans is meagre. Evans claimed that a stone he had located in the West Magazine of Knossos was a standard weight. The stone weighs 28.6 kilograms; it has carved in relief on each of the four faces an octopus, while a hole near the top makes it easy to handle with the aid of a rope. Opinion remains divided as to the function of the stone: either it was a unit of measurement or a royal anchor.

Imports to Crete fall into two main categories. First of all, there were raw materials needed by the palace workshops. Gold and silver would have come from the Cyclades or Asia Minor; attractive stones for the making of bowls and seals could be obtained in the Peloponnese; precious stones might have to travel from much further afield, lapis lazuli coming from distant Afghanistan; ivory may have originated in Syria where elephants were not extinct till the ninth century BC; plumes and amethyst were supplied by the Egyptians; while emery was available on Naxos and tin existed in Central Europe and Italy. The second category of import was luxury items of foreign manufacture. Initially they were small and exotic objects from East Asia: beads, seals, and amulets. Later Egyptian stone vases were imported along with the favoured linen, but it is likely that some of the finds on Crete represent presents exchanged by ambassadors. We know that amongst other things Egypt exported fine furniture to Cyprus, so a Minoan ruler could have been in receipt of similar goods. The sole evidence for such a transaction is an ivory sphinx found in a house at Mallia: this piece of furniture inlay dates from about 1700 BC.

Crete and Egypt

Our survey of Minoan influence overseas has often touched upon relations between Crete and Egypt. We shall close this chapter by focusing attention on the nature of this relationship.

For archaeology the contacts between Egypt and the Aegean in the Bronze Age are vital for chronology. For ancient Cretans sailing into one of the mouths of the Nile delta the experience of direct contact with Egyptian civilization must have been amazing. Here was a people that everyone recognized as the oldest in the Ancient World. Even the Hyksos occupation during the seventeenth and sixteenth centuries BC failed to disrupt the old continuity of life. At Knossos an alabaster lid was unearthed that records the name of Hyksos pharaoh Khyan as 'son of the Sun'. The Minoans kept up their trade and diplomatic contacts with the rulers of Egypt throughout the first half of the second millennium BC. They were distinguished from the 'Ha-unebu', all 'people from beyond the seas', by the special term of 'Keftiu'. This was the Egyptian name for Minos' Crete. Nevertheless, Thotmes III regarded himself as the universal monarch 'who bound the waters with his fist'. The Minoans were accorded a status not enjoyed by other maritime peoples but they remained tribute-bringers in the eyes of the Egyptians. How far tribute can be regarded as state trading at this period is impossible to say. It would seem that the Rekhmire wall-painting of Aegean envoys bearing gifts contains more than a reference to tribute. The items presented are the staples of trade: pottery, statues, metalware, copper ingots, and oil. Whilst the pharaoh reciprocated gifts with the king of Knossos, he also allowed the Egyptian people to trade with the Minoans. The economic blockade of Aegean goods that started at the close of the second millennium BC was the result of attacks on Egypt by the Greeks and other sea peoples. In the Bronze Age the Mycenaeans evidently took over from the Minoans excellent relations with Egypt.

6

Economy and Society

Transition from the Neolithic

The levelling of the settlement mound at Knossos on the construction of the first palace destroyed much of the evidence for understanding the transition from the Neolithic period to Early Minoan I and II phases. A similar situation obtains at Phaestos, where no trace of an Early Minoan phase exists at all. Despite the loss of succession levels at these chief sites, it is possible to sketch the economic changes leading up to the Bronze Age palaces.

A cave find gives a radiocarbon date of 2550 BC for the last phase of the Neolithic Age on Crete. Whether or not this represents a backward contemporary of Early Minoan I we cannot be sure. But characteristic of the final Neolithic are two-handled jars, pots with lids, and other prototypes of Minoan wares. How far these products disclose the growth of craft specialization is hard to tell. In the village economy of Neolithic times there would have been few specialists because the skills of community had not yet passed out of the reach of the individual member. Farming, building, tanning, flint-making, pottery, spinning, and weaving: these activities every household could manage. Only a reliable surplus of foodstuffs would have freed the most able exponent from the tasks of agricultural production and permitted the emergence of the craftsman. Such a person may have been the specialist potter recognized by the pattern he made on his work at the prehistoric mainland sites of Lerna and Tiryns. His sign was a hound and its quarry; he left this trademark by rolling an incised cylinder upon the wet clay. Itinerant craftsmen explain the diffusion of discoveries and techniques in the pre-palatial era, whilst the concentration of skilled workmen in the palaces accounts for the take off of the economy in the favourable conditions for international trade created by Minos' navy.

House plans are available for the late Neolithic period but not the Early Minoan I phase. At Knossos the Neolithic dwellings had many rooms and the settlement itself was of agglomerate plan. Most of the finds for Early Minoan I come from burials. Though the custom of burial in caves and rock shelters persisted strongly,

Opposite: The Priest-King or Prince of the Lilies. This relief fresco from the Palace of Minos at Knossos dates from about 1500 BC

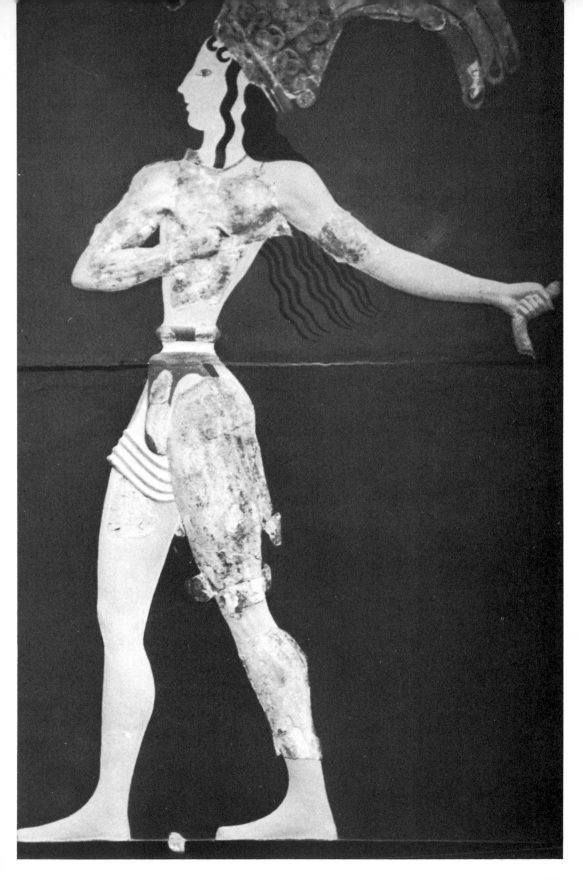

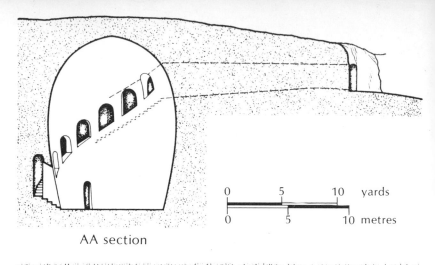

AA section

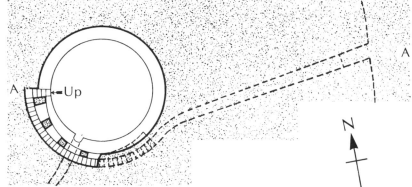

0   5   10   yards

0   5   10   metres

N

A reconstruction of the underground granary at Knossos. It was built shortly before the first palace there

the innovation of this time was the rock-buiit tomb, usually circular in plan and two metres in height. Except for a tiny piece of copper found on Mochlos, the grave goods contained no metal and were mainly pottery. Only with Early Minoan II do we encounter sealstones, stone vases, figurines, and metal objects like bronze daggers and gold jewellery. In the rich grave goods of the Mesara round tombs is apparent the high level of workmanship that one would have expected to find at Vasiliki. The mansion, or great house, of Vasiliki was a carefully laid-out complex, some 30 metres long, built of timber, mud brick, and plaster. Undoubtedly it was parallel to the Early Minoan buildings that stood on the Knossos site prior to the palaces. In these settlements we can say that a considerable degree of craft specialization had developed: it was sustained by an increasingly productive agriculture as well as improved methods of storage. From this time dates the large underground granary at Knossos. It was more than 10 metres in diameter and 15 metres in height; a staircase led down from the top for easy access. This storage chamber stands on a watershed – one side looks back over the slow economic transition from New Stone Age to Early Bronze Age, the other forward towards the revolutionary progress in material life caused by the inception of the palace economy. Above all, it emphasizes the continuity of development in Minoan Crete.

The palace economy

During the Bronze Age Crete saw a rapid and uninterrupted expansion of population, resulting in a density of settlement more than twenty times that in the Neolithic period. Renfrew puts the number of people living on the island at the time of the new palaces at 256,000, giving the territory under the direct rule of Knossos some 50,000 persons. He believes that this population would have supported the 5,000 residents of the Palace of Minos itself. Unlike other parts of the Aegean and mainland Greece, problems of security evidently did not trouble Crete and so resources were not diverted into fortifications and military works. On the contrary, the wooden walls of the island, the vessels of the Minoan navy, served a dual function before 1450 BC. The seas were patrolled to ensure that Crete was peaceful and secure; they were also rid of pirates so that merchant ships could sail safely from port to port. The importance of the latter aspect of naval supremacy was discerned by Thucydides. Writing about the location of cities, he commented:

Cities which were founded in more recent times when navigation had at length bcome safer, and were consequently beginning to have surplus resources, were built right on the sea . . . . But the older cities, both on the islands and on the mainland were built more at a distance from the sea on account of the piracy that long prevailed – for the pirates were wont to plunder not only one another but also any others who dwelt on the coast but were not seafaring folk – and even to the present day they lie inland.

Still more addicted to piracy were the islanders . . . . But when the navy of Minos had been established, navigation between various peoples became safer – for the evildoers of the islands were expelled by him and he proceeded to colonise most of them – and the dwellers of the sea-coast now began to acquire property more than before, and to become more settled in their homes, and some seeing that they were growing richer than before also to put walls round their cities . . . the weaker cities were willing to submit to dependence on the stronger and the more powerful men with their enlarged resources were able to make the lesser cities their subjects. And later on . . . they made an expedition against Troy.

As Renfrew has pointed out, this passage succinctly delineates the historical pattern of the Bronze Age. The wealth generated by Minoan trading activities gave rise to the Mycenaean hegemony which reverted to large-scale piracy in the attack on the Trojans.

The Minoans were first and last peaceful traders; quite alien to them was the belligerence of the Mycenaean Greeks. At the core of Minoan civilization was the palace household with its storage rooms, workshops, and land. The development of writing in Crete was stimulated by the complicated transactions involved in running the palaces and great houses. Even in hieroglyphic inscriptions – the earliest written form known – it is transparent that we have accounts of foodstuffs received, stored, and disbursed. Tablets from Phaestos and Knossos record such items as wheat, oil, barley, olives, figs, livestock, wine, and honey. The storage

A Linear B tablet from Knossos which records livestock kept by the Mycenaean princes occupying the Palace of Minos

capacity of the Palace of Minos alone may have exceeded 200,000 litres.

The accounts preserved on the clay tablets lead us to the view that the regulator of the Minoan economy was the palace, which acted as a redistributive centre for goods. Inventories show the far-reaching interests of the Minoan rulers; there are tallies of animals, land holdings, and lists of personnel. In the same way as the shepherd on a neighbouring hillside, a farmer down the valley from the palace, or a fisherman along the coast worked for the king, so did the skilled craftsmen in the workshops enhance the royal treasury. But it must not be forgotten that the ruler was a priest-king and the palace as much a temple as a place of residence. Tablets record payments to men and gods, ritual offerings being of ample size.

Agriculture

Minoan civilization depended economically on the cultivation of wheat, the olive, and the vine. Barley was added in the Early Minoan II phase, a shift in cereal production that may reflect either a change to a drier climate or some exhaustion of the soil.

Carbonized grain appears in the upper levels of the Neolithic settlement mound at Knossos and an olive stone in a Early Minoan I deposit near the Royal Road there, but Evans questioned whether wine was known at all in prehistoric Crete. Recent excavations have yielded numerous grape pips, whose size and shape indicate the domestication of the vine. The Early Minoan II village of Mirtos, too, has given us an open vat which could have been used for expressing the juice from the grapes. Late Minoan Gournia boasts a whole wine-producing complex, though one opinion regards its purpose as the separation of olive oil. After harvesting the olives were drenched in hot water, and pressed to extract the oil, which was separated from the water in a vat.

Olive oil was a staple commodity. Its three chief uses were for cooking, for cleaning the body, and for lighting. Linear A and B tablets document the rations of oil awarded to palace staff. Ventris also deciphered a tablet speaking of 'unguent boilers', and it seems likely that olive oil was perfumed with sweet-smelling herbs in order to make a luxury cleanser. The value of oil for illumination can be estimated from the increased number of lamps detected in Middle Minoan deposits. Like oil, the social importance of wine is

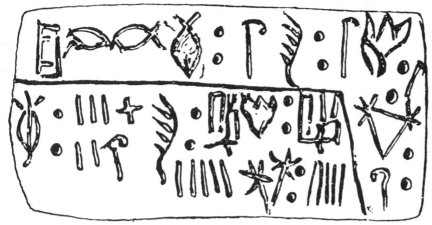

A clay tablet from Middle Minoan Phaestos which has signs for wheat, oil, olives, and figs in the top line

suggested by the growing sophistication of the utensils associated with its consumption. In the Tomb of the Tripod Hearth, for instance, at Zapher Papoura, fourteen bronze vessels used to heat beverages were discovered. Wine undoubtedly acquired a religious significance during the palatial era. Beer may have been brewed from Early Minoan times, since barley ears in relief occur on clay jugs from the Palace of Minos.

Linear B tablets at Knossos record small quantities of figs being issued for ritual offerings, along with barley, olive oil, and wine. Figs and olives appear among the trees reverenced by the Minoans, who were much inclined to pillar worship. Another gift for the gods was honey, large jars of which we know the Mycenaean dynasts sent to the sacred cave of Eileithyia at Amnisos. Besides the excellence of honey as a food, the Minoans may have found it helpful in embalming, as did the Babylonians. The practice could have inspired the curious Greek legend of Glaukos, who drowned in a *pithoi*. This son of Minos, while still a child, was playing ball one day in his father's palace, when he suddenly disappeared. With the aid of the Delphic Oracle, he was traced to a large storage jar full of honey. Minos insisted that his discoverer raise him from the dead, or be shut in the cellar with the drowned prince. When the latter course of action was adopted, the reluctant companion noticed a snake approaching the boy's corpse and, seizing his sword, he killed it. Presently another snake crept along to its dead mate with a herb in its mouth, which it laid on the lifeless scales. Slowly the snake revived and, seeing this incredible happening, the incarcerated man applied the miraculous herb to Glaukos with the same result. He and Glaukos then shouted loudly for help, until a passer-by heard them and ran to summon Minos, who was overjoyed when he opened the cellar and found his son alive.

Vegetables eaten by the Minoans included cress, lettuce, celery, asparagus, carrots, peas, and beans. Fruits were pears, quinces, and dates – perhaps the date palm came from Egypt. In the fields, vineyards, and orchards of Bronze Age Crete the ubiquitous tool was the axe-adze, an iron version of which remains a favourite

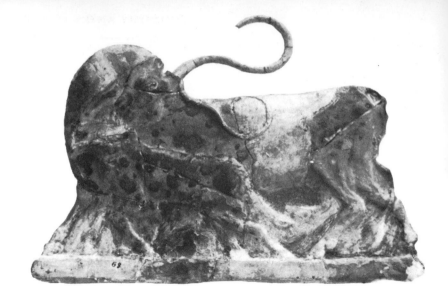

Right: A faience plaque from Knossos of a cow suckling a calf

Below: Part of the fishing tackle discovered at Gournia

on the island today. The other standard tool for cutting trees and clearing undergrowth was the double axe. The plough may have been yoked to oxen: a hieroglyph from Phaestos is a plough with a steering-handle. It does not seem that cattle were raised specifically for beef or milk production. The Linear B accounts reveal an overwhelming majority of sheep, goats, and pigs; one series of tablets at Knossos lists a total of 25,000 sheep. Livestock generally played a minor role as a food source because large flocks were kept for wool. Diet would have received supplement from the sea: fish, shell fish, octopus, and squid festoon late Minoan art and fishing tackle was recovered at Gournia by Harriet Boyd.

Metallurgy

No tin sources have been located in the Aegean. The high tin content of bronzes in the third millennium BC is accounted for by imports from Bulgaria and Romania, or the existence of local alluvial deposits of tin which were worked out in ancient times. Copper was in plentiful supply and moulds for casting were adopted in the final stage of the Neolithic period. By the Early Minoan II phase the settlement of Vasiliki possessed two-piece moulds, which allowed the casting-to-shape of both surfaces of a double axe. The fine bronze statuettes of worshippers found at Tylissos were probably cast by the 'lost wax' process, whereby a wax model encased in clay was baked in a kiln so that the wax melted and ran off leaving a mould, in which the molten bronze could be poured. The characteristic personal weapon was a short dagger with a very broad butt. In Middle Minoan times longer blades and the full sword evolved, a splendid example of which is the ceremonial one from the first palace of Mallia. It measures 101 cms and has a pommel of rock crystal. Influence from West Asia cannot be discounted, since weapons made by smiths in Crete and Phoenicia exhibit similar forms. The main defensive weapon was a huge shield with a figure-of-eight shape made of hide on a wooden frame. Like the smaller round shield depicted on the Phaestos Disc, the Minoan shield would have managed without the addition of metal.

More crucial in the progress of civilization was the new range of tools that became available to the farmer, carpenter, shipwright, builder, gem-cutter, and sculptor. Axes, axe-adzes, sickles, knives, hammers, chisels, saws, gouges, borers, awls, gravers, tweezers: these bronze tools transformed the Minoan world and provided the means of establishing the palace economies. That the Minoans were fully aware of their debt to metal is shown not only in the iconography of the double axe but even more in the copper ingot carried by one of the 'tribute-bearers' painted on the wall of the Rekhmire tomb. To the pharaoh the king of Knossos sent one of the staples of Bronze Age international trade.

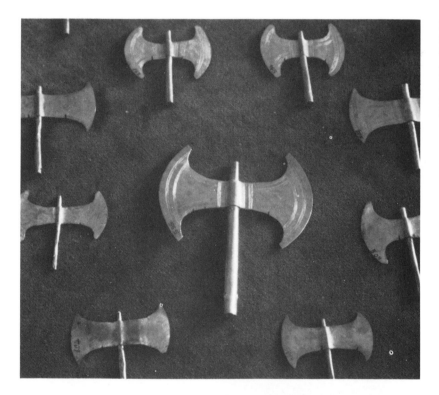

Left: Part of a hoard of gold double axes from Arkhanes

Below left: A Middle Minoan mould for casting double axes which was found at Mallia

Transport

The Bronze Age witnessed a revolution in communications. The dependence of Neolithic man on his own feet and hands seemed remote in the first half of the second millennium, when there were ox-carts, chariots drawn by horses, and sea-going ships.

On land, pack animals may have been used from the very beginning of the Bronze Age, though the first direct evidence we have comes from a Late Minoan figurine. It is a terracotta model of an ass carrying water jars. The horse is not documented until the fifteenth century BC, but horses may have reached Crete before then from West Asia or Egypt. Horse-drawn carts probably travelled on Minoan roads, the remains of whose terrace walls indicate the efforts made to improve communications. *Gephyra*, the ancient Greek name for a bridge, appears to be a Minoan word in origin. Kings and dignitaries would have ridden in the two-wheeled chariot: a model of a litter found at Knossos gives an impression of transport available for shorter journeys. The size and weight of a chariot had to be kept to a minimum. Chisels and gouges assisted in the manufacture of spoked wheels – the technique of using heat to bend wood was understood by 1600 BC – but the chariot-maker sought every means to increase the speed of the vehicle. A chariot discovered in the tomb of Tutankhamen (1352–1344 BC) even has a featherweight floor of interlaced leather thongs. The Linear B tablets draw attention to the importance of the chariot to the army of the Mycenaean rulers of Knossos after 1450 BC: more than four hundred vehicles are listed. Heavier carts of course were always available for the transport of bulky goods, as a Middle Minoan terracotta wagon unearthed by Evans proves. Neither the wagon

The Late Minoan terracotta model of an ass carrying water jars

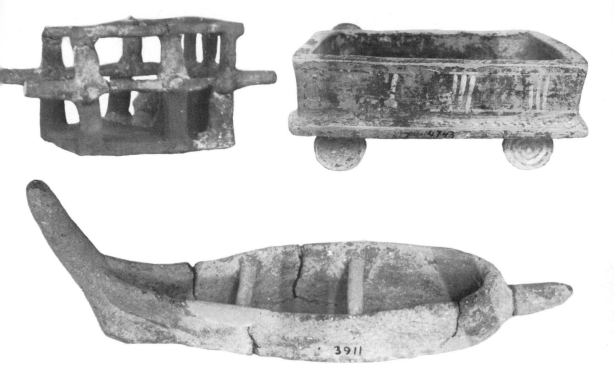

nor the chariot were of economic significance, nor were they a great aid to communication when compared to the ship. Journeys were made by sea, first along the coast, then between the Aegean islands, and finally to distant shores of the Mediterannean Sea. Typical craft possessed oars and a single mast: an average length is estimated as 20 metres. The sail may have had only a minor role because the safest method of navigation would have been to find a quick anchorage whenever a sudden Aegean storm blew up. Yet a variant of the Daedalus legend says the famous architect-engineer fled by means of newly invented sails.

Clay models of various types of Minoan transport. The litter (top left) was found at Knossos. The ship (above) and the painted wagon (top right), which dates from the end of the third millennium BC, were found at Palaikastro

Government

The palaces of Minoan Crete bear witness to the government of the island by princes. The numerous palaces and great houses flourishing before the disaster of 1450 BC suggest that there were a number of principalities over which the king of Knossos exercised some form of authority. The occupant of the Palace of Minos may have been looked upon as the chief priest-king, the spiritual rather than the temporal leader of the Minoan peoples. The road with the best terraces climbs to the shrine on Mount Juktas, south of Knossos. Up this winding roadway the king could have brought sacrificial offerings for dedication to the mother-goddess, whose epiphany on the peak of a mountain is recorded on contemporary seals. The symbol of this monarch's power was the impressive throne which Evans dug from the ground almost at the start of his excavations.

A reconstruction of the Mallia sword which has a pommel of rock crystal

At Mallia were discovered two items belonging to the regalia of the prince who lived there. Apart from the ceremonial sword mentioned above, we have a sceptre of brown schist in the form of a panther straining on a leash, and covered with an elaborate design of interlocking spirals reminiscent of stone vase patterns.

The extensive magazines of the palaces and the vast amounts of agricultural produce they stored so effectively provided the reliable basis for palace life. The rulers enjoyed a comfortable existence, surrounded by the finest domestic products of the Bronze Age, but they were never tempted to emulate the glories of their peers elsewhere. The Minoans built no pyramids, ziggurats, or acropolises: their civilization was epitomized in the palace itself.

Evans took the view that the king of Knossos ruled a maritime empire. It now seems unlikely that such a state of affairs ever obtained. Certainly the Minoan fleet enjoyed some kind of primacy, essentially perhaps a peace-keeping role in the Aegean, but there is no evidence pointing to the political control of overseas settlements, let alone other islands or the coastline of mainland Greece. Colonies of Minoan settlers on Kythera, Thera, Keos, Melos, and Rhodes pursued their own separate destinies. The link with the homeland was in terms of trade, as shown in the large quantities of pottery imported in Late Minoan times. Imperial aspirations would therefore appear to be an addition of later historians and archaeologists.

Social classes

The architecture of Minoan Crete divulges something of the social classes below the royal family. The plan of the palace itself bears witness to the existence of state functionaries as well as members of the court: it tells us that the palace was the focal point of a highly stratified society. The complexity of the organization required to control the elaborate redistribution system based on the magazines and workshops is reflected in the inscribed tablets and sealings. A bureaucracy was needed to keep check on the commodities belonging to the king. Scribes noted receipts and disbursements in the linear scripts, thus ensuring the maintenance of the social order and the continuation of the religious ceremonies. Besides the specialist craftsmen at work in the palace, there were resident priests and priestesses whose task it was to assist the ruler in his priestly functions. Though the palace was probably regarded as sacred in its entirety, the priest-king would have performed ceremonies in special rooms like the pillar crypts at certain times in the calendar. We suggest later that during the New Year festival the ruler celebrated the season of fertility with a holy marriage between himself and the high priestess, who impersonated the mother-goddess. In East Asia the king had long been looked upon as the intermediary between mankind and the gods. The Sumerian king-list even reports that kingship 'came down from heaven'.

Moreover, texts describe the king as son of a god or goddess: 'son of Enki', the water-god, 'the begotten one of the great mountain', Enlil, or 'him whom Ninlil bore', the grain-goddess. Just as Sumerian kings were anxious to insist on their divine election, Minos must have reminded his subjects of his colloquy with Zeus once every nine years. It is interesting to notice, all the same, that Plato considered this meeting to have been the source of Minos' reputation as a wise ruler and a great judge. Perhaps a connection exists between this ancient fame and the Law Code of Gortyn, the first European law-code and the only complete one from classical Greece. Although it was inscribed around 450 BC on a court building in Gortyn, a city on the Mesara Plain, it incorporates older material as well as locally established custom.

The ceremonial weapons of the ruler of Mallia, the longsword and the axe-head, have a lesser parallel in the tombs of Zapher Papoura, where elaborate bronze utensils and implements were buried with the noble dead. Further evidence of an aristocracy is equally available in the large residences that dotted the Minoan countryside. The remains of two grand houses stand at Tylissos, some 10 kilometres west of Knossos. One of them, known feebly as 'House A', was furnished with an entrance-hall in the middle of the east side; a northern service quarter with food storage and cooking facilities; a southern residential wing containing a lustral basin, a pillar-crypt, a bath, a toilet, a light-well, and several bedrooms; an upper storey offering dining facilities, a balcony, and rooms for the family. Drainage passed from room to room in stone conduits. Of the bronze cauldrons or baths stored in the building, one of them is the biggest ever found. The whole structure eloquently indicates the wealth and social status of its owners, who lived apparently before 1450 BC with no measures for defence at all. 'House A' was fired during the Mycenaean takeover and subsequently reoccupied by an invading chieftain. The Minoan residents were members of the nobility, their house and the other one in the vicinity acting perhaps as satellites of the Palace of Minos. They oversaw locally the raising of crops, the care of animals, and the well-being of the village folk.

Beneath the noble class lived the peasantry, hardly advanced beyond a Stone Age economy. Where they were attached to estates or operations under the direction of the palaces and the great houses, it is likely that they had the advantage of bronze tools and draught animals. Most village families would have possessed a piece of land on which they grew food for themselves. Unpaid labour may have been due on royal lands and a tithe on their own crops. There does not seem to have been a slave class of any significant size, unlike Greece and Rome. The absence of this degrading institution, undoubtedly the corollary of an unmartial society, is one of the notable features of Minoan civilization.

Life in the settlements clustered round the palaces was much more complicated. Hagia Triada, the harbour town of Phaestos,

A woman from one of the
Thera frescoes showing
the full skirt and short
open bodice

had a spacious colonnade of shops and offices. Though the palaces
organized the greatest share of trade internally and overseas, there
must have been scope for the enterprising trader. A merchant class
would have emerged in the peaceful conditions created by Minoan
naval supremacy. In the development of Palaikastro, a humble
neighbour of Zakro, we can discern the growth of commercial
activities. Originally a rural agglomeration, little more than a large
self-sufficient village, Palaikastro turned more and more to the sea,
becoming by Late Minoan times a prosperous community trading
with Cyprus and Egypt. The main thoroughfare, which was
paved and drained, boasted houses furnished with as many as
twenty rooms. Yet in comparison with Palaikastro, the town of
Gournia appears positively industrial. Apart from a small palace,

Elaborate hairstyles and
jewellery are shown in
this fresco from Knossos

the seat of princeling or governor, the houses are modest and
tightly packed together along narrow, twisting alleys. They were
the homes and workshops of carpenters, smiths, weavers, masons,
potters, farmers, and fishermen. Here was the most important
centre of production so far found outside the palace workshops:
Gournia may be called the Manchester of Minoan Crete.

Women

The position of women in the Minoan community seems to have
been particularly fortunate. They were not strictly segregated
from activities undertaken by men since girls even took part in the
daring bull games. The dominance of the mother-goddess in
Minoan belief meant that women were involved in rites and ceremonies, priestly associations of women being formed at palaces
and holy places. Priestesses would have enjoyed high social standing and exercised influence in courtly matters. Perhaps the queen
of Knossos as high priestess was superior in status to everyone but
her own husband, the reigning Minos.

Herodotus said that Lycia was the only Aegean country where
children were regularly named after their mothers, not their
fathers. Whilst he drew attention to the Cretan customs of the
Lycians, his account nowhere proposes that matriarchy had
derived from Crete. If matrilinear succession ever existed on the
island it had died out completely before the time of Herodotus.
Archaeology has nothing to add, save the fact that the martial
domination of the male was unknown before the arrival of the
Mycenaeans.

Dress and adornment

Before the end of the Neolithic period the inhabitants of Crete span and wove wool. Loom weights and spindle whorls appear in the settlement mound at Knossos after 4000 BC. These artefacts no doubt represent household crafts, the activities each family undertook for its own benefit, but in the Bronze Age the whole craft of textile production was clearly transformed into a commercially exploited industry. Records show the large numbers of sheep at Knossos reared for their wool, and we know that one of the gifts taken to Egypt by the 'men of Keftiu' was woollen cloth. Spouted vats found at Mirtos are possibly among the earliest ones to be used for fulling and dyeing. Very considerable quantities of murex shells discovered with Middle Minoan II pottery near Palaikastro suppose a local purple industry. And Herodotus mentions that Cretans sold purple obtained from the mollusc murex.

Bodily comfort was a priority for the Minoans. Bronze scrapers and tweezers were available in bathrooms, along with perfumed oil. Clothes were usually made from wool, though wealthier people may have worn linen garments imported from Egypt. The only examples of costume made out of animal skins occur in ritual scenes: the priests and priestesses on the Hagia Triada sarcophagus wear skins which may have come from sacrificial animals. There was much variety in ritual as well as secular dress, and the various peoples of Minoan Crete may have had different styles of clothes.

Masculine costume was essentially a loincloth tucked round the waist or held in place by a belt of some kind. It could be worn either as a kilt or a pair of shorts, when folded under the groin. During the second palatial era a stiffer loincloth became fashionable; it was cut to expose the thighs and often turned up at the back like an animal's tail. The cod-piece, straight and narrow in design, was sometimes worn with a belt alone and no loincloth. Some Late Minoan seals, however, depict a long kilt without any sign of a cod-piece. As in Egypt the men normally went bare above the waist.

For women, too, exposure of the breasts was the fashion. They dressed in long skirts with girdles wound double round the waist and knotted, their ends hanging down in front. Bodices left the breasts bare but had collars rising to a point at the back of the neck. The characteristic features of feminine costume are visible in the two faience statuettes of the snake-goddesses, or snake-priestesses, which Evans excavated at Knossos. But elaborate court dress of this kind was unsuited to ordinary occasions, and in all probability a simpler version was worn by less elevated women.

Indoors and in sacred places the Minoans went barefoot. Outdoors they wore sandals and boots, protecting their heads with small hats and their shoulders with cloaks.

Hair was allowed to grow long, with curly locks hanging down on each side of the face in front of the ears. Shaving, however, was common for men, though beards and moustaches were not un-

familiar. Women seem to have adopted fantastic hairstyles, piling their black tresses high above their heads. They also used pigments for making-up their faces.

Both men and women of all ranks liked to display jewellery. The commonest find in graves is the bead, but necklaces, hair-pins, earrings, armlets, wristlets, anklets, and other ornamental decorations were a Minoan delight. Particularly exquisite is the gold pendant of two bees heraldically arranged about a honeycomb, a piece of jewellery unearthed at Mallia in 1930. It is our misfortune that so little jewellery survives from this fashion-conscious age.

Late Minoan I bronze statuettes of male and female worshippers showing typical Minoan costume

Sports and pastimes

The bull game, discussed in the chapter devoted to religious beliefs, is the best-known Minoan sport, but we have evidence of dancing, music, board games, and boating. In the 1960s Spiridon Marinatos dug out at Akrotiri a fresco of a pair of youthful boxers. The contest of these Theran youths would have been echoed in the boxing and wrestling matches which were staged on Crete. Other frescoes he found later document a fascination in seamanship, and a variety of craft, which suggests the likelihood of regattas. We can easily imagine the ruler of Knossos at Amnisos, or his brother from Phaestos at Hagia Triada, watching rowing contests between vessels of the royal fleets.

Dancing and singing had a ritual as well as a secular purpose. Ariadne was the marvellous dancer of Greek legend and her dancing place may well have been the Theatral Area in the Palace of Minos. On Delos a tradition was preserved that Ariadne gave Theseus a statue of the mother-goddess and that the figure of the labyrinth was danced by the rescued youths and maidens as the statue was being set up. The dance of the Lady of the Labyrinth was therefore performed beyond the shores of Crete: it was a ceremonial branch of one great parent religion which in prehistoric times flourished in the Aegean. It is not possible to determine the moment when secular dance was recognized. Spectacle and entertainment were incorporated in ancient religion; the Minoan worshipper could perceive the spiritual aspects and appreciate the technical mastery at the same time. He lived in a world still uncomplicated by sharply defined gods and goddesses.

The debt of the Greeks to Bronze Age Crete in terms of dance and music is recognized in folklore. At Delphi on the first occasion on which the hymn to Apollo was sung to the lyre, the performer came from the island. In the lowest levels of the Minoan palaces there are remains of musical instruments, notably pipes, whilst the lyre and the double pipe were in use throughout the palatial period. Also recovered from these sites are ivory gaming-pieces in the shape of a bull's leg and a lion's head; Knossos itself provides a draught-board nearly a metre long, made of ivory plated with gold and inlaid with rock crystal and faience.

Left: The young boxers from Akrotiri on Thera

7

Art and Architecture

Painting and Pottery

The labyrinthine impression of the Palace of Minos on an ancient visitor was reinforced by long corridors which led unexpectedly into spacious well-lit rooms with amazing fresco decoration. The alternation of dim passageway and bright chamber, the half-glimpsed jars of the palace stores, and the strong colours of the timber sections and downward-tapering columns, must have persuaded the newcomer that he was inside an elaborate mansion, the homely residence of a priest-king, rather than a monumental palace staffed by hierarchies of priests. There was no striving after the eternal: cult rooms discreetly opened from ground-floor courtyards, usually as pillar crypts, and the deities they contained were not beings, but symbols of elemental powers. Minoan religion was concerned to preserve the closest possible links between man and the natural world, an approach to the cosmos that gave rise to the unique style of palace architecture and decoration.

The painting of walls on Crete is known from the beginning of the old palaces (c. 2000 BC). Traces of frescoes have been recovered in palaces, houses, and villas, but it was probably not until the era of the new palaces (c. 1700 BC) that geometric designs gave way to naturalistic representation. The vast majority of surviving Minoan frescoes were made in the century prior to the disaster of 1450 BC. They are true frescoes; artists painted on wet plaster, working quickly as the plaster dried out. Their vivid colours derived mainly from mineral substances – blue, silicate of copper; white, hydrate of lime; red, haematite; yellow, ochre; and black, carbonaceous shale. The frescoes vary in size, according to the area of wall available, and occasionally the scene painted has been modelled in very low relief on the plaster. Subjects indicate the popularity of the bull games as well as the prominence of women in Minoan society. The most elaborate fresco at Knossos was painted on the walls of the Corridor of the Procession and in the South Propylon. Originally it may well have been composed of hundreds of gift-bearers – handsome, long-haired youths wearing ornaments and loincloths.

Opposite: The fresco of gift-bearers from the Palace of Minos

Recent excavations on the island of Thera at Akrotiri have produced remarkable examples of Minoan-style frescoes. These wall-paintings depict young boxers, monkeys, antelopes, luxuriant landscapes, fishermen, and sailors. One miniature frieze, over 6 metres in length, is said by its excavator, Spiridon Marinatos, to narrate the story of an expedition in a sub-tropical landscape, presumably Libya. Scenes bring to light a fleet of warships, several towns, soldiers, herdsmen, women, children, and wild animals. This visual chronicle, now in the Archaeological Museum in Athens, may be a record of international events during the Cretan supremacy.

Pottery in the Early Minoan period was handmade, but at settlements like Vasiliki and Mirtos wares were already attractively decorated and complex in shape. As we saw earlier, Evans took advantage of ceramic development to construct the first chronology of Minoan civilization. The fast potters' wheel could have reached Crete from Egypt or Asia Minor in Middle Minoan IA. After 2000 BC only the largest jars were normally made by hand. The introduction of the wheel allowed the indigenous tradition of pottery to achieve splendid results, in the palace workshops at Knossos and Phaestos especially. The old palaces saw the perfection of polychrome Kamares ware, which received its name from a cave on Mount Ida where it was first unearthed. The finest specimens were for use in the palaces and sometimes they sought to imitate metal shapes and ornamentation. Characteristically Kamares ware had a shiny glaze, its decoration being white and red on a dark ground. The new palaces provide us with naturalistic motifs, in the painting of walls and vases, but it is the 'marine style' of decoration for pottery that still intrigues the observer today in the Archaeological Museum at Iraklion. A pot may be covered with octopuses, argonauts, starfish, rock, and seaweed.

Faience and ivory

In earliest times in Egypt the technique of faience modelling was practised. The method consists of preparing a core of quartz grains by cementing them together, and then adding an alkaline glaze during the process of firing. Faience was commonly used by the Minoans for beads and pendants and in the palace workshops for statuettes, vases, and plaques. Coloured plaques of houses dating from the eighteenth century BC have been found in a deposit at Knossos. They may have served as inlays decorating wooden furniture or a wooden chest. Evans obtained much information on Minoan buildings from these tiny ornaments: they made possible his 'reconstitutions' of parts of the Palace of Minos. The well-known statuettes of the snake-goddesses or snake-priestesses also discovered at Knossos bear witness to the incredible skill of the faience-maker. Combined together in these ritual objects are the mysterious power of the divinity and the natural proportions of its

Opposite: A flask painted with an octopus – a favourite decoration of the 'marine style'. It was discovered at Palaikastro and dates from about 1500 BC

Faience insets from Knossos. These early representations of Minoan houses helped Evans in his rebuilding of the Palace of Minos

everyday manifestation in women and serpents. Though we shall consider the religious implications of these snake-clad figures in the next chapter, it is worth noting here that surviving images lend weight to the view that Minoan religion was never anthropomorphic. The divinities represented were but aspects of a divine nature that encompassed the entire world.

An outstanding ivory-carving is the so-called snake-goddess presently on display in the Boston Museum of Fine Arts. The authenticity of this ivory and gold figure has been questioned, but many scholars believe it to be contemporary with the faience snake-goddesses. Considerable numbers of ivory figurines have been dug up at Knossos – subjects range from bull leapers and animals to plants and divinities – and it appears that the craft had its own long traditions on Crete. The ivory itself was imported either from West Asia or Egypt.

Stone vases and seals

Minoan craftsmen were expert in the manufacture of stone vases. The availability of metal tools – saws, chisels, awls, punches, to name the ones in general supply – had a beneficial effect on all craft industries, but for the worker of stone the new drills and cutters opened the way to intricate exterior decoration. By the end of the old palaces it is evident that Crete was a major exporter of stone vases.

The earliest vases were made of chlorite or chlorite schist. Later the local stones in use were marble, gabbro, gypsum, limestone,

A lid of green steatite found at Mochlos. An Early Minoan II example of the stone-carver's art

and serpentine. Imported stones included Egyptian alabaster and Aegean obsidian. From the numerous finds it is possible to understand the process of manufacture. The piece of stone was first blocked out by pounding and chiselling; then the inside was hollowed, the cutting being done by an abrasive powder fed into the hole; finishing and polishing the outside was achieved with oil, after the incised or relief decoration had been applied.

Stone vases were commissioned for domestic, ritual, and funerary purposes. An early favourite was the bird's-nest vase, so-called on account of its shape. Ritual vessels could be represented by the delicate rhyton of rock crystal which was found in the sanctuary of the Zakro Palace, though the most famous libation vessel is the bull's-head rhyton found by Evans in the Little Palace at Knossos. Carved from black serpentine, the bull's head, measuring 30cms, possessed inlaid eyes and nostrils as well as golden wooden horns. Liquid was inserted into the rhyton through a hole at the top of the neck and poured through the mouth on to the altar. Other bull's-head libation vessels have come to light on Crete, along with a vessel in the form of a lioness.

Seal-engraving was an art of particular appeal to the Minoans. As a means of security and signature seals were in demand even before the foundation of the first palaces. Apart from such a utilitarian role, seals were also credited with magical properties and acted as the ancestors of the 'milkstones' prized by modern Cretan women. A seal-stone was an amulet, a talisman against evil, and a lucky charm. For this reason we have to exercise caution in the interpretation of seal-engraving. In some cases the subjects are

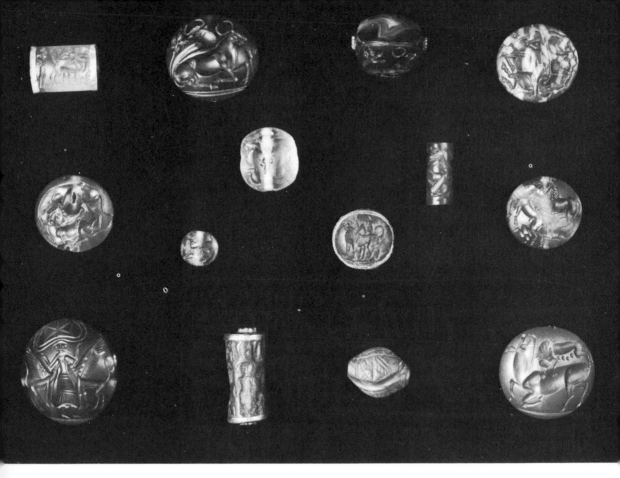

human beings, animals, plants, and ships, in others geometrical designs and characters of the hieroglyphic script. Occasionally we encounter a religious scene or a spectacular moment of the bull games. Throughout the palatial period engravers made seals of remarkable beauty as well as fine signet-rings in bronze and gold. The naturalism of painted pottery and frescoes was reflected in these designs along with the infectious sense of joyous adoration that typified late Minoan civilization.

Jewellery

Already in Middle Minoan IA craftsmen were producing pieces of gold jewellery that matched the growing sophistication of pre-palatial society. Some of the best jewellery comes from exploration of the circular tombs on the plain of Mesara. Though the antecedents of these early pieces go back ultimately to Egypt and West Asia, the Minoans soon adapted the technique of working in thin sheet gold to their own purposes. For the rulers of the palaces goldsmiths made the bee pendant taken from the burial house at Chrysolakkos near Mallia, which is dated between 1700 and 1600 BC. The bees were soldered heraldically together at the heads and tips of their abdomens and their legs cradle a honeycomb which, like the eyes and abdomens, were decorated with granulations. As

144

The bee pendant found near Mallia

was suggested in the previous chapter, this pendant may be connected with the funerary myth of Glaukos, son of Minos, who drowned in a jar of honey but was later revived, and also the golden honeycomb which Daedalus wrought for the shrine of Aphrodite at Erice in Sicily. Daedalus presented his perfect honeycomb to the goddess as an offering from one who had found safety and hospitality in a strange land. Honey itself always featured in the offerings to divinities at Knossos.

The treasure of gold jewellery acquired by the British Museum in 1892 from the island of Aegina could well have been Minoan in origin. The pieces, similar to the bee pendant, were probably plundered from the Mallia tomb. One of the ornaments consists of an embossed ring in the form of a two-headed snake, inside of which are a pair of collared greyhounds and a pair of monkeys eating. From the ring hang chains, ending in alternate discs and flying owls. Originally eight carnelian beads completed the design.

Building materials and construction

The building materials available to the Minoans were those in general use throughout the Bronze Age. They were stone, wood, lime mortar, clay, and reeds. Where the Minoans advanced architecturally on their Aegean neighbours was the extensive application of dressed stone to palaces and houses. The bronze saws and chisels which became available just before 2000 BC were indispensable for this work. Other important Minoan innovations were the practice of building to a height of several storeys, the use of pillars and columns, piped water supply, elaborate drainage systems, and indoor toilets.

The facing-stone so freely employed in palace construction was alabaster, a fine-grained, marble-like variety of gypsum. With bronze saws 2 metres long, Minoan stonemasons were able to saw this soft stone into sheets over 2 metres square and often little more than 3 centimetres in thickness. These alabaster veneers could then be fitted to conceal a wall of inferior material. In the vicinity of Knossos there were quarries full of all kinds of gypsum: the slightly soluble blocks used for interior walls, the water-resistant slabs for bathrooms and lustral basins, and the smooth, lustrous sheets for dressing. Quarries also existed near Phaestos and Hagia Triada.

Limestone served the builder best wherever there was exposure to the open air. Outside stairways, pavements, and courtyards were always constructed with limestone. Dressed blocks were used for pillars, pillar bases, door and window facings, and walls. At Mallia local sandstone took on this role.

Bronze Age Crete abounded in forests – in Roman times it was believed that the island was the native place of the cypress – and wood was lavishly employed in the palaces. Wood provided columns, ceiling, and roof beams; flooring for the upper storeys; stairs, door, and window frames; doors; and frames to strengthen mud-brick walls. The remains of tree trunks found by Evans in the Royal Villa north of Knossos suggest an original width of 0.80 metres, a very large piece of timber indeed.

Unlike the Egyptians, the Minoans did not prepare gypsum mortar, but a lime mortar, composed of lime, sand, and gravel. They knew how to make true cement by adding the volcanic ash of Thera. Plaster was applied to stone and mud-brick walls, reeds probably acting only as a backing for ceilings. Bricks made of clay assisted in the building of the upper storeys of palaces and houses, since they helped to reduce the weight of walls. Water pipes were also made of clay but there were no tiles for the reason that the Minoans favoured flat roofs.

Little attention was at first paid to foundations. At Mallia buildings were erected upon exposed surfaces of rock and the western wing of the Palace of Minos managed with a few layers of small irregular stones. The prevalence of earthquakes, however, obliged the Minoans to strengthen foundations, the most notable example being the sealing of earlier ruins of Phaestos with a heavy layer of concrete. The houses at Tylissos were also given a rubble base that went down to bedrock. Walls varied according to the type of building: there were rubble-filled walls dressed with stone on the outside of palaces and mansions; wood-framed walls of adobe brick assisted in the construction of upper storeys and doubtless formed

A fresco of columns at Knossos. It shows the typical Minoan shape with shafts that taper downwards

the staple for less elegant houses; and solid masonry was often used for interior walls. The frequent practice of facing all types of walls with a layer of plaster, sometimes painted, added to their strength – particularly in the case of the walls of loose rubble.

Columns were both decorative and functional. They set off courtyards and staircases, while their use within rooms allowed the construction of large ceremonial areas. Pillars, square in section rather than circular, bore much of the weight of the upper storeys but in the tiny pillar-crypts their presence must be seen as purely ritualistic. Here they were built as sacred symbols, not structural supports.

Roofs were never very heavy. Their probable method of construction was a framework of wooden beams on which thatch was laid and covered with tamped impervious clay. They had a slight slope for drainage but all evidence to date points to a Minoan preference for horizontal roofs.

Palaces

On Crete the most recent archaeological exploration has centred on the recovery of the Minoan palace at Zakro. Like Mochlos and Pseira, the site was never reoccupied after the fire of about 1450 BC. In its main essentials, the small but excellent Zakro Palace resembles the plans of the three larger palaces at Knossos, Phaestos, and Mallia. The central courts of these palaces, orientated roughly north to south, acted as the organizing nuclei of layout and the arena for the ritual bull sports. In the central courts of Mallia and Zakro surviving stones may have been the bases of altars. Like the Palace of Minos, the Zakro Palace had its cult and ceremonial rooms as well as its storage facilities situated in the western wing, while the royal suite was placed across the courtyard in the eastern wing. In one of the storerooms inscribed clay tablets had been kept in wooden boxes of which only the bronze hinges remain. To the north of the apartments occupied by the royal family there was a large bathroom or lustral basin. The royal suite itself opened eastwards on to a colonnade flanking the side of a court, in the middle of which stood a circular spring chamber which may have been roofed. Close by a square spring chamber appears to have been accessible only from outside the palace. A well also in the eastern wing was certainly used for offerings of olives in the final days of the palace. Possibly we have here at Zakro a palace incorporating a sacred spring or even a number of sacred springs. The

**The palace
at Zakro**

1 North Entrance
2 South Entrance
3 Central Court
4 Altar
5 Royal Apartments
6 Spring with
   roof (?)
7 Spring Chamber
8 State Rooms
9 Cult Rooms and
   Palace Archive
10 Magazines
11 Workshops
12 Kitchen with
   dining-hall above

northern wing contained the kitchens on the ground floor and a dining-room above as well as a main entrance: the southern was a two-storey block which appears to have housed the workshops.

The model for palace construction could well have been the Palace of Minos. The pillared hall next to the north entrance at Knossos seems to have had a dining-room above it like the kitchen at Zakro. Unfortunately both northern and southern wings of the Palace of Minos have been destroyed by erosion and quarrying for stone in later times. As we observed in the first chapter, the outstanding remains are the magazines and cult rooms of the western wing and the extensive royal quarters of the eastern wing. The great staircase – a unique architectural feature in the Bronze Age according to Evans – constitutes the centre-piece of the latter. It once connected no less than five storeys, two above the ground level of the central courtyard and two below. Built round a light-well, the majestic stairway had two flights per floor and rested on large tapered columns of painted wood. Each storey ended in a colonnaded verandah overhanging the small river that flows along the eastern aspect of the palace. The main chamber of the Hall of the Double Axes opened on a spacious colonnade to both the east and south. Evans was able to undertake the reconstruction of the staircase because it remained complete and practically undamaged long enough after the abandonment of the palace for it to be silted up with debris and earth. Destruction by fire at Knossos is most obvious in the western wing.

The lustral basin adjoining the Royal Apartments at Zakro

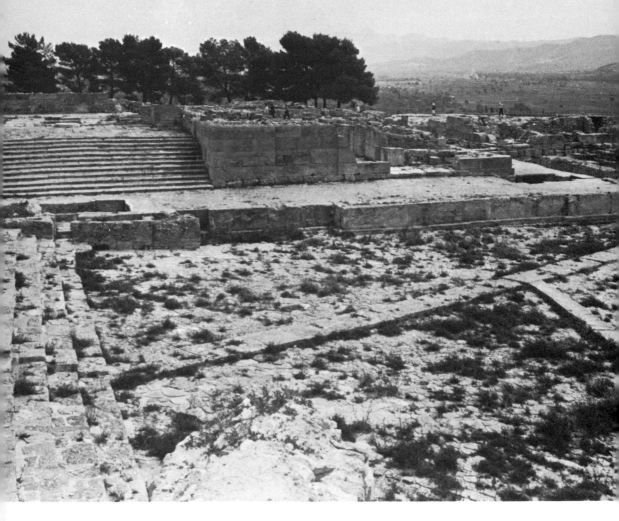

Erosion of the hillside at Phaestos has taken its toll of palace buildings too. Much of the eastern and southern wings has disappeared, so that the layout cannot be completely envisaged. Nevertheless what remains can be divided into magazines, cult rooms, ceremonial halls, royal living quarters, guest rooms, service areas, workshops, courtyards, and entrances. The main approach was from a paved court on the west as at Knossos, though the wide stairway, the huge columns, and the large light-well belonging to this entrance were unusual. To the north of the monumental entrance and at the same level was a colonnaded court rather like the cloisters walked by medieval monks. It has been suggested that the court was laid out as a private garden for the royal family, whose apartments ran along its northern side. At Phaestos the rulers dwelt in the northern wing of the palace, doubtless to enjoy the wonderful panorama of the mountains beyond. Like Knossos, toilet facilities were built into the royal suite.

At Mallia the ground plan reveals storage facilities in the eastern and western wings; workshops in the northern wing; cult and ceremonial areas in the western wing; and residential quarters in the north-western corner of the palace and in the southern wing. Like Phaestos, the Mallia Palace had a colonnaded central court with several entrances.

Houses

The sole exception to the rule that Minoan houses were square may be the 'oval house' at Chamaizi, midway between Gournia and Palaikastro. As its interior walls were set at right angles, the suggestion has been made that the house was given an oval wall outside in response to the site on the crown of a hill. Nicolas Platon, however, argues from the remains of an altar, idols, and ash deposits that it was a peak sanctuary. The so-called well in the inner court, he points out, would neither collect nor hold much water and would be far more suitable as a sacred rubbish pit. This interpretation is an attractive one for the Middle Minoan IA building, which has no parallel in domestic architecture.

A large but somewhat crudely built house at Sklavokampo came to the attention of archaeologists during road works undertaken in 1930. Though the design was original and pleasing, the materials used in construction failed to reach the usual standard of the Minoan country mansion. Exterior walls were undressed stone; inside, there were neither wall-paintings nor paved floors; and staircases were wooden, not stone. The design itself consisted of a main entrance, spacious living-room, cult room, verandah, guest rooms, and toilet beneath the stairway leading to an upper storey. The magazines and servants' quarters surrounded a light-well and possessed a separate entrance. Communication between the two parts of the house was probably by means of a service-hatch, now lost.

Some 8 kilometres east of Sklavokampo, in the middle of the little town of Tylissos, lie the remains of two very fine houses. A third building, known as B, seems to have acted as a storehouse. They were first excavated by Joseph Hazzidakis between 1909 and 1913. Buildings A and C, the residences, had much of their walls either dressed with stone or covered with painted plaster. House C, the smaller one, is best preserved, many of its walls still reaching to the second storey. It has an irregular outline with groups of rooms forming projecting wings. One group in the south-east contained a pillar crypt, another in the west the storage rooms; in the north were the living quarters, and at the centre several rooms of unknown purpose. The main hall of the residential wing had a flagged floor and a pier-and-door partition, reminiscent of palace arrangements. Nearby was a bathroom and at the end of a corridor giving access to the stairs, a toilet provided with a drain through the outer wall. The upper storey appears to have had a large hall

The western approach to the palace at Phaestos

Left: Part of one of the
substantial houses at
Tylissos, west of
Knossos. A cistern and
supply channel for water
can be seen in the centre

Below: A staircase
belonging to one of
the houses excavated
near Zakro

sited over the storage rooms. The owners of the Tylissos houses were certainly members of the Minoan aristocracy, possibly cousins of the rulers of Knossos. Around 1450 BC the buildings at Sklavokampo and Tylissos were fired, and only the latter was reoccupied by Mycenaean conquerors.

Of interest is the villa with the lily-frescoes at Amnisos, the port of Knossos and the location of the cave sacred to Eileithyia. The villa was once an elegant residence, neat in design and well built. Outside walls were dressed with limestone slabs, while the interior was finished in gypsum and painted plaster. An ample hall, with a six-bayed pier-and-door partition and delicate wall-paintings of lilies, opened on to a flagged terrace with a fine view of the sea and the island of Dia, where Ariadne died. The two-storeyed villa was destroyed sometime after 1500 BC. Fire played a part in its demolition, but the dislodging of the heavy stone foundations could have been caused either by an earthquake or a flood-wave of exceptional violence.

Town houses varied according to the prosperity of their inhabitants. Workaday Gournia possessed few houses of any size and the palace there was diminutive even by the standard of modest Zakro, but around the big palaces and in the trading port of Palaikastro there were substantial private buildings. Particularly well preserved is the ground plan of House Da at Mallia. This 'well-to-do' residence had two storeys with flagged floors downstairs. There were storage rooms, big living-rooms, a bathroom, and a toilet, besides a single entrance.

A restoration of House Da at Mallia; seen from the north-west

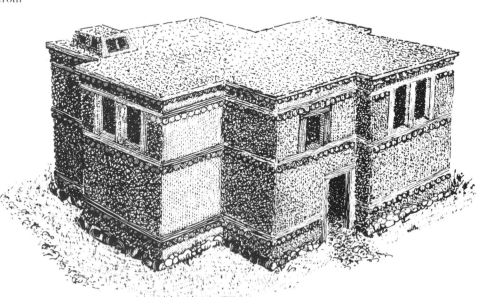

Tombs

To the Mesara Plain we must turn in order to understand the
Minoan tomb. Yet our knowledge of the circular burial chambers
situated there is very limited indeed. Their origins are much
disputed and their place in architectural development during the
Bronze Age is not entirely clear. In *The Tombs of Mesara* Keith
Branigan has argued recently that the Mesara tombs were the
prototype of the *tholoi* of the Late Bronze Age. He notes the
uncovering of a *tholos* tomb at Arkhanes, south of Knossos, in 1966.
This tomb, dated as Middle Minoan II, was constructed about a

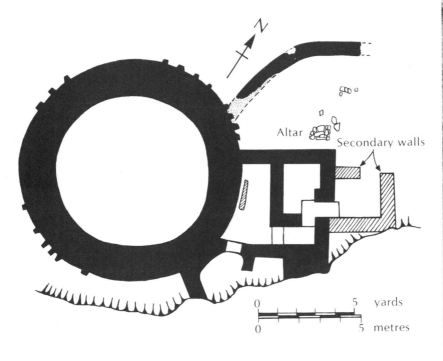

Altar

Secondary walls

0   5   yards

0   5   metres

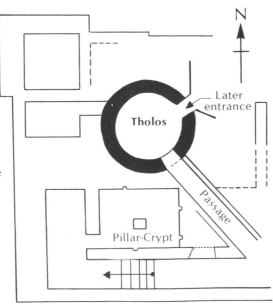

Later
entrance

Tholos

Passage

Pillar-Crypt

Above and right:
The plans of two circular
burial chambers: the large
tholos at Kamilari (top)
and the Middle
Minoan II complex at
Arkhanes (right)

Opposite: The view out
on to the Mesara Plain
from Phaestos

century before the earliest *tholos* tomb yet discovered on the Greek mainland. It possessed a circular chamber, whose south-east entrance was approached by a long corridor. To the north-west of the chamber, and built on to it, were three rectangular rooms, while to the south were more rooms and a pillar crypt. Branigan sees this tomb as a descendant of the Mesara tombs and suggests that it was transitional between them and the circular burial chambers soon to appear in Messenia on the Peloponnese.

The Arkhanes tomb apart, there seems to have been a slow but steady movement away from circular chamber tombs in Middle and Late Minoan times. The immemorial custom of communal interment, found in Neolithic cave sites and rock-shelter tombs, had resulted in the construction of the Mesara round tombs, which were often placed in small groups of two or three. This arrangement may reflect a tribal or clan structure in pre-palatial society, though the number of small ossuaries also found suggest the building of family vaults. While the round tombs were still used in the period immediately after 2000 BC, the tendency of Minoan communities to adopt the practice of individual burial in clay jars and containers becomes quite evident during the era of the palaces.

Round tombs appeared first on the plain of Mesara in Early Minoan I. Their sudden appearance and their concentration in southern Crete recommended to Evans the idea of an immigrant people arriving from Libya early in the third millennium BC. He was convinced that the Mesara tombs were imitations of circular houses with oblong antechambers, and he thought that these, and the tombs which copied them, were of North African provenance. Doubt was cast on this hypothesis in Evans' own lifetime and today scholars hold that there are important differences of both materials and techniques between Libyan and Egyptian burial chambers and those which were erected on Crete. Most likely as an explanation for the origin of the circular chamber tomb is a local development from artificial cave tombs. About the Mesara there were comparatively few caves available for burial purposes so that increased population might account for early tomb construction. Archaeological exploration of other parts of the island, the un-surveyed west and the north-west in particular, may well produce further evidence of the transition from cave to tomb.

On the Mesara the round tombs are free-standing. They were built on the ground, or had their floors sunk a metre below the surface. Only a few tombs indicate the possible development from rock shelters. It is rare to find an example of the use of a natural rock overhang. The sophisticated use of building stone, however, is soon apparent, the pieces facing the wall of the tombs being very carefully worked. At Kamilari, west of Phaestos, most of the stones in a big tomb had a properly cut face and were cut to the shape either of a rectangle or a wedge. Strength was obtained by having stones large enough to span half the width of the wall. The Kamilari tomb is thought by some archaeologists to have had a

Opposite: Part of the treasure of Minoan jewellery which was discovered on the island of Aegina

stone vault, but we cannot be sure the roof was not finished in thatch or mud-bricks. It comprises a circular burial chamber, several anterooms, and an enclosure for an altar stone. Grave goods taken from the tomb include stone vases, terracotta ware, statuettes, and beads. A dramatic clay model shows four dancers holding hands in a ring, inside horns of consecration. Their dance might have related to the worship of the mother-goddess as Ariadne, the divine dancer. The Minoan soul beseeched her aid in the difficult steps of the dim passage through the underworld. Ariadne was probably a *psychopompos*, a 'leader of souls'.

Continuity of population is one of the strongest impressions which emerge from the study of Minoan tombs. Later burials were individual affairs but they represent no break in cultural tradition. They did not abandon the prehistoric Mediterranean idea of the cave-like sepulchre, which found its most impressive form in the palatial architecture of the Temple Tomb, south of the Palace of Minos. This royal burial place covered a large area with several rooms and had a rock-cut chamber for interments; it could date towards the end of the Middle Minoan period.

Left: A Late Minoan vase with a stylized leaping dolphin

Opposite: Two elaborate vases in the Kamares style from Phaestos

8

Religious Beliefs

Our knowledge of Minoan religion is derived almost entirely from the material remains of the civilization. Neither Linear A nor Linear B offers an insight into the religious beliefs of Bronze Age Crete before the Mycenaean invasion. There are references to deities in both scripts – indeed the use of Linear A would seem to have been devoted to ritual purposes – yet we are unsure as to the name of a single Minoan deity. The present analysis has to rely on an investigation of those objects that can be reasonably supposed to have had a religious significance. The absorption of Minoan beliefs in Greek religion, one of the consequences of the Mycenaean takeover of a more developed culture, does allow a degree of comparison, but there are dangers in interpretation by analogy and the ideas expressed in this chapter must be regarded as speculative.

In Minoan civilization flowered the genius of the prehistoric Mediterranean world. The Minoans never seem to have been a nation; only their skill as seafarers, a reputation forever linked with the name of Minos, brought them into contact with peoples outside of Crete. To these strangers the Minoans may have appeared as members of a unified culture. They were probably not. Bronze Age Crete was inhabited by a mixture of peoples, speaking different tongues: the differences in speech alone would have given rise to local variations in custom and outlook. Minoan civilization was able to accommodate this diversity and find its own characteristic form through the development of the palaces. Within these unusual buildings, at once the centres of spiritual and temporal power, the priest-king or his representative undertook duties for the benefit of men and gods. Whatever happened in the palace rituals, the Minoan peoples would have had their own ways of worship. At this time religious beliefs had not yet fixed on anthropomorphic divinities, but remained close to the elemental powers and processes we now call Nature. Gods and goddesses had not emerged in solely human shape. The ancient Cretan saw spirits everywhere; he perceived in the tumbling stream or the sporting dolphin or the fluttering dove the very movements of the divine spirit. The universe lived. Its vitality was manifest in countless aspects: sky and sea, mountains and hills, trees and flowers,

Opposite: The 'poppy goddess' from Gazi. This Late Minoan III statuette hints at the use of opium on Bronze Age Crete, since the poppies reveal the incisions necessary for the extraction of the drug

An Early Minoan
mother-goddess
from Mochlos

animals and men. And all of these were caught up together in the
great movements that modern man knows to be earth tremors and
volcanic eruptions.

Yet the prevalence of earthquakes seems to have had more effect
on palace architecture than on religious beliefs. In Minoan religion
there is a conspicuous lack of anxiety about death. As Platon said of
the remarkable exhibits in the Archaeological Museum at Iraklion,
'A hymn to Nature as a Goddess seems to be heard from everywhere, a hymn of joy and life.'

Divinities

In the quotation cited above, Platon connected the zestful spirit of
Minoan art with the only deity who, we can be sure, was reverenced by the Minoans. She is the mother-goddess, the goddess of
fertility worshipped throughout East Asia, Egypt, and the Aegean
in earliest times. In other metamorphoses the Minoan goddess was
Inanna, Ishtar, Mylitta, Astarte, Cybele, Isis, and Aphrodite. A
seal from Knossos provides us with a portrait. The mother-
goddess stands on the peak of a mountain, which is flanked
by two lions. In the background we can descry a mountain
sanctuary and a male suppliant. Evident is her relationship to
wildness and the life of animals, snakes, birds, and fishes. The
Greek cult of Britomartis is instructive as this goddess bears an
ancient name meaning 'sweet maid'. In mythology she is pursued
by Minos and is assimilated with the huntress Artemis, in whose
presence beasts and plants would dance. A gold ring from
Mycenae, which may be of Cretan workmanship, shows another
aspect of the power of the mother-goddess: fecundity. At the
season of first-fruits she sits beneath a sacred tree adorned with
poppies and holding her full breasts. Female worshippers
acknowledge her authority in front of a double axe, which Evans
believed was her sacred symbol.

Worship of the mother-goddess was introduced into the Aegean
with the earliest farmers, and the cult would have only been

Below left: The seal
from Knossos which
shows the
mother-goddess on a
mountain peak

Below right: The gold
ring from Mycenae
showing the mother-
goddess as the symbol
of fecundity

A Middle Minoan III
faience statuette from
Knossos showing either
a snake-goddess or a
snake-priestess

strengthened by later emigrants from Asia Minor and through
commercial contacts with East Asia and Egypt. Simple images of
her are found throughout the islands. On Crete she adopted the
distinctive Minoan dress of ample skirt and bare-bosomed corset.
This was probably invented for the goddess and was a ritual dress
before it became a costume of ceremony. However, there is a
danger in assuming the omnipotence in Minoan religion of a single
deity. As Martin Nilsson long ago cautioned in his study of the
Minoan-Mycenaean faith, the Knossos mountain seal could be a
representation of a mistress of animals rather than the fertility
goddess of East Asia. A plurality of divinities may have existed.

The problem of identification besets us again with the two
faience statuettes from the Palace of Minos. It is uncertain whether

they represent a priestess or a goddess. Both of them are associated with snakes. One statuette has three serpents coiled around the figure. The head of one she holds in her right hand, its body curls up the arm, goes behind her shoulders, and then descends her left arm. About the hips and breasts two more serpents decorate her attire. The other statuette holds out a small snake, tail upwards: the missing left arm most likely ended with a second snake. Here we encounter a familiarity with reptiles that is certainly prehistoric in origin. Among the Greeks we know that women celebrants carried snakes in their hands, a Dionysian practice that lasted into Roman times. The Minoan statuettes might therefore relate to a similar ceremony. The serpent is an arcane symbol of earth and water: like a river winding its way, the serpent creeps silently along the ground; it dwells in the earth and issues forth like a spring or a new shoot from its hole. Above all the serpent can penetrate the tomb, and in sloughing its own skin epitomize the resurrection of the dead. The Greeks regarded the serpent as a representative not only of the dead but also of the gods. When Daedalus was trying to dispose of the corpse of Talos, whom he had killed in a fit of jealousy, he pretended to passers-by that in his sack he was piously carrying a dead serpent, as Athenian law required.

Carl Kérényi has gathered together the pre-Greek indications that foreshadow the cult of Dionysos. He argues persuasively that the Minoans worshipped under an unknown name this god of bulls, snakes, wine, and women. His sacred vessel would have been the bull-headed libation cup, brimming with heady wine. It is perhaps worth recalling the chthonic aspect of Dionysos perceptible in a Greek story of his birth. Serpentine Zeus coiling with Rhea, who had transformed herself into a snake to avoid her son's advances, begot Persephone, the wife of the underworld god Hades. Then again the writhing sky-god mated, but with his daughter Persephone, who bore Dionysos on Crete. To the Greeks, Dionysos was a foreign deity of incredible power – the Thebans refused his worship and were driven to legendary madness and murder. Dimetor, 'twice-mothered', was an epithet he acquired in another birth story that would make him son of Zeus and Semele, daughter of Kadmos, the Phoenician king of Thebes. Archaic tales of sacred snakes recur in Greek mythology: even in Olympia, Zeus took the place of a serpent. But the most famous account of a Greek god supplanting an indigenous snake-god concerns the Oracle of Delphi. From this shrine Apollo, the son of Zeus and Leto, expelled Python, slaying the creature next to the sacred chasm in the temple of the earth-mother. In the *Hymn to Apollo*, which was probably composed in the eighth century BC, Apollo commands the sailors from Knossos to become priests of his cult. They sail to the Corinthian Gulf, and near the foot of Mount Parnassos they found a shrine of the god. The legend points to a Cretan genesis for the reverence of Apollo Delphinios, who appeared as a dolphin, and notable too is the fact that in Hittite-Luvian the pre-Greek word Parnassos means 'shrine'. On the slopes of this holy mountain Apollo first fought Python.

In the Europa myth the snake marriage is replaced by love for a bull. Although Zeus took the guise of an extraordinarily handsome beast, it would be foolhardy to say that there was a Minoan bull-god, despite the horns placed on altars. Kerényi proposes the incorporation of the bull in the cult of the pre-Dionysian deity, so that Pasiphae and Ariadne are mother-daughter dualities like the Greek goddesses of Eleusis, Demeter and Kore. In this context the Minotaur, half man, half bull, is a manifestation of a dying god: his death is like that of the sacrificial animal representing a suffering, dismembered deity. Perhaps the mysterious formula recorded by early Christian writers dates from this era: *taurus draconem genuit et taurum draco*. 'The bull is the father to the snake and the snake to the bull.'

It was St Paul who remembered all Cretans were liars when he landed on Crete. The reputation for deceitfulness had been earned because of Cretan legends about Zeus. The Greeks could accept that 'the father of gods and men' was born and brought up on the island, yet in no measure could they understand the notion of his burial there. The 'immortal' of Greek tradition would not quite square with the Minoan pattern of a dying and rising god. Like Adonis, this Minoan Zeus may have been the consort of the mother-goddess. In Byblos the temple of Astarte celebrated the annual resurrection of Adonis on the blooming of the red anemone.

Sacred symbols

The double axe, known as the *labrys* from the name current in Asia Minor, was the supreme symbol of Minoan religion. It may have signified the mother-goddess, as Evans believed, because the double axe is never seen in the hands of a god, but only appears as a sacred tool in her cult. *Labrys* is obviously connected with *labryinthos*, yet scholars have argued that the double axe must be the symbol of the thunder-god, the Minoan Zeus. According to this view, the double axe is the representative of the sky-god, his thunderbolt: thus we have the sky-father fertilizing the earth-mother, whose symbol becomes the horns. Though it is almost positive that Zeus Labraundos was a Hellenized version of the Hittite weather-god, who carried a double axe in one hand and a lightning bolt in the other, there is no evidence to support the claim, notwithstanding the possibility of Luvian influence on Crete.

The *labrys* was originally the sacrificial axe. In time the double axe assumed a sacred importance of its own: the divine spirit inhabited it, making the bronze implement the image of the divinity. However, its exact sacrificial role in Minoan Crete cannot be easily established. The trussed bull on the Hagia Triada sarcophagus has been stabbed in the neck, its blood streams down into a jar beneath

The great double axes
from Knossos which are
now in the Iraklion
Museum. The exact
ritual significance of
this sacred shape
remains uncertain

the slaughtering-table. Two goats lie nearby awaiting their turn as ritual offerings. Apparently uninvolved physically in the letting of blood stand two double axes in socketed bases. We consider the bull games as a sacred rite in a later section, but here it should be said that we are uncertain as to the practical function of the *labrys* in Minoan religion. The nearest parallel is a Greek rite performed on the island of Tenedos, in which a bull calf played the role of a suffering god and the sacrificer was punished. On this small island off Troy, a new-born calf was dedicated to Dionysos and the man who struck it with a double axe was stoned by the people, till he reached the sea.

Besides the ritual double axes found in shrines and sacred caves archaeologists have recovered a number of strong double axes in association with tools like chisels and saws. This is why we should be careful not to take every find as having had a religious significance. Nevertheless, the widespread distribution of the *labrys*, as a sacred symbol, implement and weapon, does serve to remind us of the very foundation of Minoan civilization – the use of bronze. Without bronze saws and chisels the stonemasons would have been unable to build the great alabaster-veneered palaces. Had not Daedalus' jealousy of Talos been raised to fever pitch when his young nephew invented the saw by copying the jaw of a serpent? Possibly the double axe was reverenced by the Minoans as a divine gift. The Sumerians had seen the pickaxe as the chief gift of Enlil, the god of the earth and the air. Enlil gave the Sumerians this implement to assist in the construction of cities including his own residence of Nippur.

Entangled with the double axe are the horns of consecration identified by Evans. Horns decorated the roofs of shrines as well as altars. In shrines the *labrys* seems to have been placed between the horns, along with libation jugs, boughs, and other offerings. No consensus of opinion has been reached on the meaning of the sacred horns. While one school of thought would compare them to symbols of mountains, which were assuredly reverenced by the Minoans, another suggests that they derived from the horns of the sacred bull. To complicate the issue further, we know that the Egyptian mother-goddess Isis was shown with a solar disc and cow's horns when identified with Hathor. It is therefore not impossible that both the double axe and the horns symbolized the Minoan mother-goddess.

We are on firmer ground with the devotion accorded to pillars and trees. Not only have we the innumerable votive offerings around the stalactites and stalagmites of Cretan cave sanctuaries as testimony, but more the prominent position of the pillar in Minoan architecture bears witness to the symbolic purport of the column. It is probable that the palaces were regarded as sacred in their entirety, though particular rooms served for cult purposes. Among the places of worship at Knossos were the pillar crypts in the Palace of Minos, the Little Palace, and the Royal Villa. Elsewhere the ancient visitor to these buildings would have been conscious of the red column broadening towards the top; the support of a complex structure and the symbol of an unbreakable cord that joined men to the soil, the seed-bed as well as the death-bed of life. Minoan beliefs were not oppressive. They were easy and friendly, a response to the abundance of material goods available on Bronze Age Crete, but they remained realistic, accepting apparently without fuss the inevitability of death. All in due time returned to the womb of the earth-mother.

Evans first drew attention to the Minoan cult of the column, whether as a standing stone, a pillar, or a tree. He also noted the large number of Mycenaean examples of pillar worship. What he sought to make intelligible was a fetishism stretching back to the Stone Age. Impressive rocks must have caught the imagination of early man just as did the hand axe he wielded so effectively in his

daily struggle for existence. Where he dwelt in caves, or like the Minoans buried and prayed in them, he often encountered the fantastic natural columns caused by the deposit of carbonite of lime. In addition to the awe of the stalactites and stalagmites he could not but feel, there was the unconscious symbolism of procreation. The cave of Eileithyia at Amnisos provides an indisputable example of a phallus in the form of a solitary stalagmite: it rises gracefully in the inner enclosure of this Greek goddess of childbirth.

Two sacred symbols of Minoan religion are found together in a votive colonnade with birds. This miniature clay shrine from Knossos consists of three pillars with beam-end capitals, each surmounted by a dove. Bird epiphanies usually relate to the mother-goddess, though in some instances they may express the presence of a household divinity. What a contrast there is between the quiet indication of the divine spirit in Minoan art and the grandiose monuments of the pharaohs and the kings of Syria and Mesopotamia. The Minoans never seem to have lost contact with the natural processes, finding always in the wildness of a cave or the splendour of a mountain-top a talisman against priestly rigmarole. The dove, if we remember the doves of Aphrodite, would have been the emblem of love and fertility. The raven perched on the top of the double axe on the Hagia Triada sarcophagus undoubtedly referred to the nether world. It reveals the

Above: The terracotta bird and pillar epiphany from Knossos

Opposite: Mount Juktas seen through the monumental horns of consecration at Knossos

two aspects of the mother-goddess: light and darkness, life and death, the antithetical, paradoxical nature of divinity. Our misfortune is that we lack a key to this record of so ancient a cult scene, which contains symbols fundamental to Minoan thought.

Birds and snakes are the creatures most favoured as cult objects. From the few remains that have come down to us though, it is impossible to draw inferences that would exclude the presence of something that is not represented. The Minoan artist may have exercised professional judgment in the choice of sacred symbols. The distinction between artistic taste and religious awe is hardly perceptible after three and a half millennia. Yet the pre-eminence of the serpent in Minoan and Mycenaean religious belief cannot be gainsaid. In 1969 Lord William Taylour uncovered at Mycenae a small storeroom jammed with clay objects, including lamps, vases, human statuettes, and 'snakes with heads raised, coiled up in a naturalistic manner, unlike anything found before on the Greek mainland'. He informed the readers of *The Illustrated London News* of the Minoan antecedents of these cult figures, and noted that previously 'snakes occur in close association with the goddess or in groups, particularly in Crete, but never, as it were, in their own right'. Maybe these serpent idols connect with the pre-Dionysian deity postulated by Kerényi. Definitely they substantiate a widespread cult of the household snake in the Bronze Age.

Places of worship

Unlike the Greeks, the Minoans carried out their devotions in unaffected surroundings. They eschewed the public temple – the columned building inevitably associated with Greek religion – choosing instead to build shrines in caves, on mountain peaks, near springs, or at home. Except for certain funerary rites, which appear to have taken place in the pre-palatial period hard by rock-built tombs, there is nothing to suggest that worship was conducted at any other places.

The Knossos seal of the mother-goddess mentioned above shows a peak sanctuary. Horns of consecration are just as clear in fragments of a carved stone vase on display at the Archaeological Museum in Iraklion. A man sets a basket with sacrificial offerings down on a round rock in front of a shrine, while possibly two other worshippers bear gifts. The largest and most impressive Minoan shrine was on Mount Juktas, whose peak is visible from the Palace of Minos. Evans explored the site in 1909, reporting an extensive enclosure as well as a shrine building with a plaster floor. The list of mountain sites where traces of sanctuaries have been found has grown tremendously since that date. But the modern visitor to Crete cannot be unaware of the Christian adoption of ancient high places, since tiny white churches settle bird-like on hilltops the length of the island.

The sacred cave of the Minoan kings of Knossos was on the

The reconstruction of the steatite vase in the Iraklion Museum which suggests a Minoan peak sanctuary

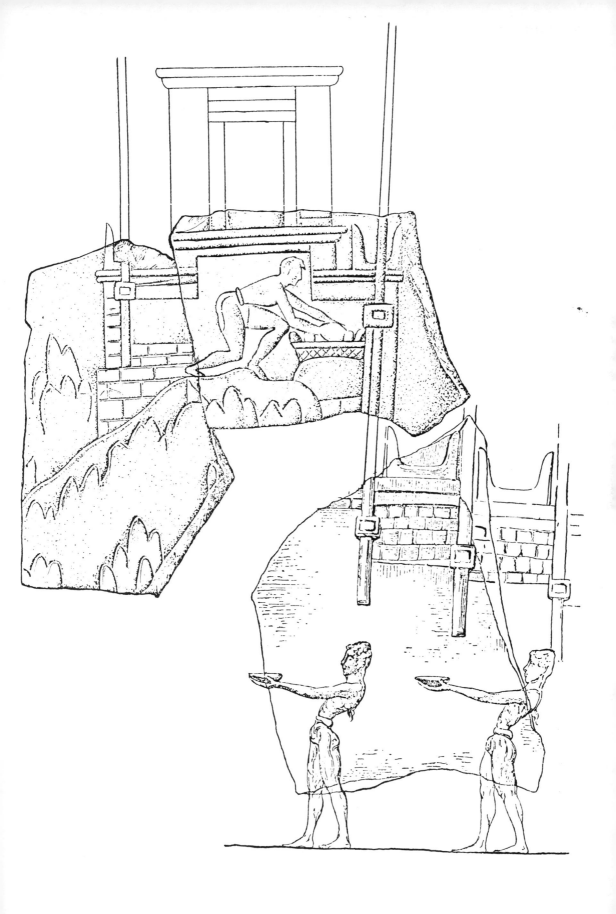

plateau of Skotieno, according to Evans. There are many caves at this location, about 10 kilometres north-east of the Palace of Minos, and the largest of them, replete with stalagmites and winding galleries, was visited from the Middle Minoan period onwards. To Skotieno Minos could have gone every nine years to confer with his divine father, the Cretan Zeus. Better preserved in the Cave of Psychro is the altar, a structure of roughly squared stones about 1 metre high. Surrounding this unadorned place of offering Hogarth discovered pieces of libation tables and cups dating from throughout the Bronze Age.

Sacred springs were of less moment except perhaps at Zakro. We know of one rock-cut spring-house, but the best surviving example is the small shrine within the Caravanserai at Knossos. Here a little niche was prepared to receive some form of sacred symbol or image.

At home the Minoans worshipped in simple shrines. The Shrine of the Double Axes at Knossos, though of late construction, was probably not untypical. It consists of a small room with a bench at the back on which stood tiny clay figures of divinities, together

A model of a cult scene from the large tomb at Kamilari: it is possible that the figures represent a sacrificial rite for the deified departed

with two horns socketed to receive either double axes or branches. Vases on the floor before the bench may have held offerings of food and drink. A circular offering-table, a clay tripod, was cemented into the floor. Besides the pillar crypts and the open spaces that may have seen sacred games and dance the Minoan palaces coped with little more than a number of one-room shrines. Even the town shrine at Gournia, a porchless room away from the palace, and the shrine building at Mallia can be regarded as late additions. So perspicacious was the outlook of the Minoans that their daily lives remained in harmony with the divine spirit: they were awed but never unintelligent.

Rites and ceremonies

In the *Laws* Plato understood the nine years of Minos to mean that the king was accustomed to foregather with Zeus every nine years and that he derived his wise government and lawgiving from these meetings. The line in the *Odyssey* reads: 'The mighty city of Knossos wherein Minos ruled in nine-year periods, he who held converse with mighty Zeus.' Homer does not say whether a Minos ruled for nine years, or for other nine-year periods as well. The poet is equally unhelpful about the frequency of 'converse' with the god, though the philosopher assumed that father and son met at regular, though distant, intervals. We cannot therefore be quite sure as to the ritual function of these important meetings: had they a connection with the enthronement of a Minoan ruler? Were they part of a pattern of royal observances designed to propitiate the divine powers? Or did they relate to some spiritual aspect of sacral kingship only dimly remembered? Possibly the last proposition is the closest to the true meaning. Minos was after all the son of a god. His relationship, even partnership, with the divine parent was a spiritual one. As priest-king and divine offspring, Minos ruled on behalf of both gods and men. His wise government – the dazzling civilization enshrined in the palaces, mansions, houses, towns, and villages of Bronze Age Crete – came from the insight he possessed, a quickness of the spirit that was renewed by personal contact with the deity.

According to the small dialogue *Minos*, a work of uncertain Platonic authorship, the meeting-place of Zeus and Minos was a cave. Perhaps to one of the Skotieno caverns the king of Knossos repaired, laden with sacrificial offerings. In the recesses of the cave, the subterranean world of the immortals, whose timeless presence in the configuration of the rock only Minos could know, there would have occurred secret ceremonies and rites. What these were we cannot tell, since the king alone would have participated for a brief moment in this experience of eternity, but it is easier to guess at some of the royal duties within the palace.

At Knossos the Minoan priest-kings appear to have performed their chief functions in the Throne Room, which had a bath for

Above: A drawing of the gold ring from Knossos which shows a woman greeting a descending male figure

Opposite: The smaller of the pair of Middle Minoan III faience statuettes found at Knossos. The other is shown on page 163

lustration. Either here or in the Domestic Quarter, where several rooms offer the possibility of ritual use, Minos would have celebrated the *hieros gamos* rite, a holy marriage between himself and the mother-goddess, represented by a priestess, who also may have been the queen. This sacral coupling at the time of the New Year festival was intended to guarantee the prosperity and safety of Minoan Crete. During the festivities the priest-king would have impersonated the divine consort, his own father the Cretan Zeus, and clad in sacred attire approached the goddess in her sanctuary. The mother-goddess, anointed with sweet-smelling oils and clad in special clothes, then welcomed her royal bridegroom. doubtless to the sound of music, the swelling note of pipe and voice.

In East Asia texts speak of effective government, good vegetation, abundant prosperity, victory, and success as resulting from the *hieros gamos* rite. Above all the idea of fertility predominates. What we have at Knossos is a local variation of the ancient cult of the dying fertility-god. The annual death and rebirth of the Minoan king, perhaps expressed by his visit to a cave sanctuary, would bring the priest-king into line with the ceremonies elsewhere known to have been associated with the mother-goddess and her consort. In Sumer the deceased husband of Inanna was said to return 'from the river', drawn forth by the lamentations of his devotees. On a gold ring from Knossos a woman with a hand half-open greets a small male apparition which floats down from a country shrine. Could not the scene refer to the cycle of birth, death and rebirth of the Minoan fertility-god? Could this be the god's return after the budding of leaves and the ripening of fruits?

The matter cannot be resolved. There seems to have been a Minoan cult of the mother-goddess, the guardian of love and fertility. We can only presume that it had features similar to those in neighbouring lands. With the bull sports we are as ill-informed, though it does appear that these rites were unique to Crete. Many ancient peoples respected the bull as a symbol of strength and

Left: The Late Minoan I
ivory bull leaper found
at Knossos

Opposite above:
The famous bull-leaping
fresco at Knossos

Right: The agate seal
showing an acrobat
apparently bull-leaping
off a platform

Opposite below: A detail
from the Hagia Triada
sarcophagus showing
gifts being brought to a
dead man who stands
on the right outside
his tomb

fertility; its size, powerful grace, and potency impressed men for
thousands of years. Yet for the Minoans the creature had a special
significance because it was the centre of a daring and dangerous
game which may have been considered holy. Frescoes, vase decoration, seal engravings, and statuettes give us glimpses of the acrobatic performers involved in the bull sports. They were young
men and women: at least the Theseus myth is correct in this
respect. They were, however, neither fodder for the beast nor
armed combatants. These youthful bull-leapers played games
with the sacred bull, probably in the central courtyards of the
palaces. Evidence of post-holes at Mallia suggest that fences were
put up for the event; the barrier was not adequate to keep people
out of the Central Court, but it was sufficiently narrow to keep a
large animal in. At Mallia and Zakro a stone base has survived in the
central courtyard too. An altar stone in the bull enclosure would
well accord with the religious nature of the sport, and, from the
point of view of performance, could supply a jumping platform.
Such a use is hinted at on an agate seal presently in the Ashmolean
Museum. It shows an elaborately decorated stone on which a large
bull is resting its forefeet. Above the bull's head a tiny acrobat
starts to somersault.

Left: The superb Late Minoan I or II bull's head rhyton from the Little Palace at Knossos. The inlet hole is in the neck and the spout in the mouth

Opposite above: A Late Minoan II terracotta figurine of a bull found at Phaestos

Opposite below: A Middle Minoan III terracotta rhyton from Pseira

Objection has been made to the feasibility of the Minoan bull-leap. It is said that the somersault depicted on the famous fresco at Knossos is a physical impossibility. No one could seize the horns of a charging bull and not be thrown off balance, let alone accomplish a full somersault. A number of alternatives have been put forward – that the performer leapt above the horns of the bull by tucking up the legs; that somersaults and handstands were achieved across the bull's back; that a jumping-off point was used. Whatever the methods employed by the toreadors, and there was most likely a variety, the danger of being seriously gored remained. Unarmed performers could only handle an enraged bull through a rare combination of personal bravery and athletic prowess. The question of their willing participation is one that cannot be decisively answered, though we are inclined to think that human sacrifice was never intended in this ceremony. The bull-leapers assisted in a sacred rite that began with the capture of a wild bull by hunters and ended with its slaughter on the altar stone of a palace courtyard. Perhaps we are back again to the precursor of Dionysos: the bull sports may have been the beginnings of his sacrificial cult.

Unreliable though the Theseus myth is in detail, it does insist that the fearsome encounter between the bull-monster and the tribute youths and maidens took place at the centre of the labyrinth, which we now recognize as the Central Court of the Palace of Minos. Before turning our attention to the other public spectacle of Minoan religion, namely dance, a word is required on the labyrinth. The Greeks identified either the ruins of Knossos or one of the numerous Cretan caves as the labyrinth penetrated by Theseus. A complex meander pattern decorating a ground-floor corridor of the palace at Knossos led Evans to believe he had solved the riddle. He discovered the remains of a pattern which ran in only one direction, towards a courtyard framed in seven columns. Kerényi has explored the ancient connotations of the labyrinthine enclosure, the dwelling-place of the Minotaur, and he emphasizes the notion of a spiritual journey. The labyrinth, whose linear form is the meander, represented a difficult passage; it was a confusing path, hard to follow without a thread, but, provided one was not devoured at the mid-point, it led surely, despite twists and turns, back to the start. The journey was not necessarily horrible, even though it passed through a place of death. Peril only awaited those pilgrims who were confined forever in the meanders and spirals. They became the prey of the bull-headed, man-eating Minotaur, a monster conceivably akin to the Egyptian hippopotamus-god Am-mut, 'eater of the dead'. The souls of deceased Egyptians were thought to be judged by Osiris and his forty-two assessors with the aid of a scale on which the jackal-headed Anubis weighed each one against the feather of truth. For the unfortunate waited the ravenous jaws of Am-mut. The nearest trace we have of a Minoan soul-eater could be the seal of a horned spirit from Mochlos.

A dancing ground at Knossos the Greeks also spoke of as a labyrinth. This is not surprising when we recall the involvement of Ariadne in Theseus' exploit; she gave the Athenian hero a way of safely negotiating the perilous passage. And the builder of her dancing place was none other than the builder of the labyrinth: Daedalus. It would seem that Ariadne, 'utterly pure', was an aspect of the mother-goddess, the Lady of the Labyrinth, when she danced on the sacred floor. But the role the princess played in the killing of the Minotaur as well as in her own death on the island

Another model of a cult-scene with dancers from the large tomb at Kamilari

More details from the Hagia Triada sarcophagus. A bull is being sacrificed on the left, and a woman is pouring libations on the right

of Dia, opposite Amnisos, is wreathed in mystery. One Greek tradition even makes Ariadne the wife of Dionysos. Legend would thus designate her as the Minoan great goddess – the divine mother and wife.

In the labyrinthine ceremonies held in the palaces, as well as the secret rites performed in caves and on mountain tops, we can discern an attempt at transcendence. Minoan worshippers sought to imitate the unimpaired vision of their king face-to-face with the deity. To assist in this spiritual quest they may have taken opium, a drug that appears as an epiphany of the goddess on a bell-shape statuette from a country shrine at Gazi. The poppies rising above the goddess' head actually reveal the incisions necessary for extracting the drug. Linear B tablets from Pylos and Knossos testify to the fact that poppies were widely cultivated both in Crete and the Peloponnese. The eating of poppy-seed cakes, however, is not the same as partaking of a narcotic for religious purposes. If the Minoans did use opium, and there seems no reason to rule out the possibility altogether, then it is certain that the habit disappeared after the Dorians invaded Crete.

The cult of the dead

Burial on Bronze Age Crete was an uncomplicated business in comparison with the tomb architecture of neighbouring civilizations. Provision was made for the honoured dead in terms of sacrifice and dwelling-place, but archaeologists have discovered nothing like the extravagant mortuary buildings of the Egyptians, a people with whom the Minoans were in close contact. For this reason the *tholos* tomb at Kefala on the Isopata ridge north of Knossos appears as an intrusion of Mycenaean burial customs. And there is little doubt that this tomb with a circular stone-built chamber sunk deep into the ground was commissioned on mainland lines by a Greek chieftain. The only Minoan burial chamber of any splendour is the so-called Temple Tomb, to the south of the Palace of Minos. The practice of communal interment descended from the Neolithic was largely undisturbed till Middle Minoan times, as is shown in the labyrinthine compartments of the clan tomb at Chrysolakkos near Mallia.

The gloomy underworld of the Greeks may have had no place in Minoan cosmology. The twittering shades of Hades, as they are described in the *Odyssey*, would have been baffled at the idyllic existence of the heroes who dwelt with Rhadamanthys in Elysium. On the contrary, the Minoan dead, whether interred in a cave, a jar, a sarcophagus, or the corner of an ossuary, could expect a satisfactory after-life. There is no sign in the material remains of the civilization of a preoccupation with mortality; the mystery and portentousness of dissolution was not so much ignored as looked upon as a natural thing. The land of the dead fused in the Minoan mind with the rich soil from which the plants and crops grow. Bereavement was an acknowledgement of the place that man had in universal growth and decay, the timeless rhythm of the great goddess and her lover, the dying god.

Our chief document of Minoan religious beliefs concerns the cult of the dead. It is the remarkable stone sarcophagus of the fourteenth century BC from Hagia Triada. Unfortunately this coffin was painted so late that it reveals Egyptian influence. Apparently the dead man stands in front of his tomb, while men bear gifts and women pour libations to the sound of the lyre. The model barque carried by the first man could be a Minoan version of the ship in which the Egyptians supposed the dead to travel. Likewise, the corpse is reminiscent of the mummy held erect by Anubis in the Egyptian ceremony of the opening of the eyes prior to judgment. The remaining illustrations on the sarcophagus are less affected by foreign ideas, and the bull sacrifice before the sacred tree is decidedly Minoan in spirit. Though the exact meaning of the iconography may forever stay obscure, it seems not unreasonable to say that we observe a rite of deification of the departed man, who has gone to the last resting place within the full bosom of the mother-goddess. The distinction between mortal and immortal, between flesh and spirit, does not seem to have exercised the Minoan mind. In death the individual followed the well-trodden path of the Cretan Zeus, whose tomb only the Greeks could not accept as authentic.

A labyrinth on a clay tablet found at Mycenaean Pylos. For the Minoans, this arcane symbol probably represented the journey to the last resting place

Epilogue:
the End of
the Minoan World

The six centuries of the Minoan palaces, an age of advanced civilization, was ended by the Mycenaean Greeks. The invasion of about 1450 BC, barely a generation later than the eruption of Thera, destroyed all the palaces save Knossos and left the towns around them as partial ruins. People drifted back to Phaestos, Hagia Triada, and Mallia, but their rebuilt houses did not equal the former standards of construction. How different the situation was from the peacefulness and stability of the Minoan period. Though the rulers of the palaces had had to cope with severe earthquakes about 1700 BC, the creative genius and technical ingenuity of the peoples they governed ensured that the civilization was not diverted from its own distinct course. New palaces were constructed and the unaggressive nature of the Minoans continued to express itself in the arts and in architecture. Minoan society was remarkably stable and ties remained firm, as the long enduring habit of communal burial bears witness, while the settlements established overseas on Kythera, Thera, Melos, Keos, and Rhodes appear to have been a response to population pressure and the needs of commerce rather than imperialist ventures. The general absence of fortifications on Minoan Crete unequivocally suggests a high degree of mutual tolerance among its Bronze Age islanders.

The Mycenaean conquerors changed all this. The Linear B tablets document their preoccupation with war and the legendary expedition to Sicily may be a memory of a disastrous sea-borne adventure which they launched. Crete suffered and Minoan culture disappeared. Knossos, the one surviving palace, was sacked about 1375 BC. Whether the rebellious islanders or rival Mycenaean lords should be blamed for the destruction, we cannot tell. That an attack on the palace came from mainland Greece is not unlikely. Under the leadership of an aggressive Mycenaean Minos the island may have become a dangerous new force in Greek politics and trade, especially if the Sicilian campaign was an historical happening.

Our understanding of the post-Knossos era is poor. Some revival of Minoan styles occurred in pottery but they were mostly simplifications of favourite motifs of the fifteenth century BC.

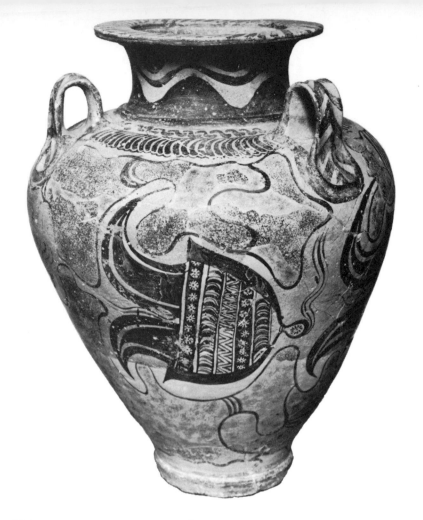

Although Crete experienced a limited revival of prosperity, the archaeological record is scant, the main site being Karphi, a mountain-top settlement over 1,000 metres above sea-level and some 25 kilometres south-east of Knossos. The small town, apparently inhabited from 1150 to 1050 BC, had only two large buildings, a Mycenaean-type *megaron* and a temple with terracotta goddesses. Another late site, Gazi, a few kilometres west of Knossos, has also produced similar figures, including the epiphany of the goddess crowned with incised poppies.

About 1200 BC Crete was settled by further groups of Mycenaeans, possibly refugees from the troubled Greek mainland. Then about 1100 BC the Dorians assumed control of the island and Minoan civilization was relegated to the obscurity of legend. Its material traces were no longer visible: they had to await the arrival of their excavator, Sir Arthur Evans, three millennia later.

This Late Minoan jar found near Iraklion is decorated with a stylized boar's tusk helmet. This type of armour was worn by the Mycenaean invaders who dominated Crete from about 1450 BC

FURTHER READING

BLEGEN, C. W.   *Troy and the Trojans*, New York, 1963

BRANIGAN, K.   *The Foundations of Palatial Crete*, London, 1970

—— *The Tombs of Mesara*, London, 1970

BURNS, A. R.   *Minoans, Philistines and Greeks*, London, 1930

CADOGAN, G.   *The Palaces of Minoan Crete*, London, 1976

CHADWICK, J.   *The Decipherment of Linear B*, Cambridge, 1967

—— *The Mycenaean World*, Cambridge, 1976

EVANS, A. J.   *The Palace of Minos*, London, 1921–35

—— *Scripta Minoa* I and II, Oxford, 1909 and 1952

GEORGIEV, V.   'The Decipherment of the Inscription of the Phaestos Disc', *Balkan Linguistics (Balkanskoto Yezikoznanie)*, XIX, 2 Sophia, 1976

—— 'The Two Languages of the Cretan Inscriptions in Linear A', *Balkan Linguistics*, VII, I, Sophia, 1970

GLOTZ, G.   *La civilization égéenne*, Paris 1923; translated as *Aegean Civilization*, London, 1926

GRAHAM, J. W.   *The Palaces of Crete*, Princeton, 1962

GROENEWEGEN-FRANKFORT, H. A.   *Arrest and Movement: An Essay on Space and Time in the Representational Art of the Ancient Near East*, London, 1951

HIGGINS, R. A.   *Minoan and Mycenaean Art*, London, 1967

HOOD, S.   *The Home of the Heroes: the Aegean before the Greeks*, London, 1967

—— *The Minoans: Crete in the Bronze Age*, London, 1971

HOOKER, J. T.   *Mycenaean Greece*, London, 1976

HUTCHINSON, R. W.   *Prehistoric Crete*, Harmondsworth, 1962

HUXLEY, G. L.   *Crete and the Luwians*, Oxford, 1961

KERÉNYI, C.   *Dionysos: Archetypal Image of Indestructible Life*, Princeton, 1976

KOBER, A. E.   'Evidence of inflection in the "chariot" tablets of Knossos', *American Journal of Archaeology*, 49, 64–75, Princeton, 1945

—— 'Inflection in Linear Class B: I Declension', *American Journal of Archaeology*, 50, 268–76, Princeton, 1946

—— 'The Minoan Scripts: fact and theory', *American Journal of Archaeology*, 52, 82–103, Princeton, 1948

MARINATOS, S.   *Excavations at Thera* I–VI, Athens, 1968–74

—— and HIRMER, M. *Crete and Mycenae*, London, 1960

NILSON, M. P.   *The Minoan-Mycenaean Religion and its Survival in Greek Religion*, Lund, 1950

PAGE, D. L.   *The Santorini Volcano and the Desolation of Minoan Crete*, London, 1970

PALMER, L. P.   *A New Guide to the Palace of Knossos*, London, 1969

—— *Mycenaeans and Minoans*, London, 1965

—— and BOARDMAN, J. *On the Knossos Tablets*, Oxford, 1963

PENDLEBURY, J. D. S.   *The Archaeology of Crete*, London, 1939

PLATON, N.   *Crete*, London 1975

—— *A Guide to the Archaeological Museum of Iraklion*, Iraklion, 1955

RENFREW, C.   *The Emergence of Civilization: The Cyclades and the Aegean in the Third Millennium B.C.*, London, 1972

SCHLIEMANN, H.   *Mycenae*, London, 1878

VENTRIS, M.   'Introducing the Minoan Language', *American Journal of Archaeology*, 44, 494–520, Princeton, 1940

—— and CHADWICK, J. 'Evidence for Greek dialect in the Mycenaean archives', *Journal of Hellenic Studies*, 73, 84–103, London, 1953

WILLETTS, R. F.   *Everyday Life in Ancient Crete*, London, 1969

—— *The Civilization of Ancient Crete*, London, 1977

ACKNOWLEDGEMENTS

The Publishers wish to thank the following for granting permission to use their illustrations. Ashmolean Museum, Oxford: pp. 19 (bottom), 38, 44–5 (all), 133. Peter Clayton: pp. 10, 22–3, 27, 31, 34, 56, 67, 83 (top), 84 (right), 89, 100, 105, 124, 126 (top), 127 (both), 129 (all), 135 (both), 143, 150, 157, 162 (top), 168. Ekdotike Athenon: p. 142. The Estate of Sir Arthur Evans: pp. 29, 122, 130. Sonia Halliday: pp. 6, 28, 36, 46, 55, 166, 178. Robert Harding: pp. 83 (bottom), 140, 159, 172, 181, 182. Harissiadis Agency, Athens: pp. 8–9, 76, 163. Hirmer Fotoarchiv: pp. 13, 59 (bottom), 95, 145. Iraklion Museum: pp. 90, 171. Mansell Collection: pp. 40, 41 (both), 70, 84 (left), 111, 121, 139, 177 (left), 179 (top), 183, 186. National Museum, Athens/ Hirmer Fotoarchiv: pp. 117, 132, 136. Photo-resources: Frontispiece, pp. 15, 18 (both), 19 (top), 20, 26, 30, 35, 53 (top), 54, 59 (top), 62, 65, 71, 72, 74 (bottom), 92 (top left and bottom), 93 (both), 113 (bottom), 147, 149, 152 (both), 158 (both), 160, 175, 176 (both). J. Powell: p. 144. Ronald Sheridan: pp. 17, 50, 53 (bottom), 60, 92 (top right), 113 (top), 114–15, 116, 118, 126 (bottom), 155, 169. University of Cincinnati: p. 75 (top). Mrs L. Killick: p. 74 (top).

Illustrations pp. 68, 104, 177: Andrew Kay. Map and plan artwork: D. P. Press Ltd.

Whilst every reasonable effort has been made to find the copyright owners of the illustrations in this book the publishers apologize to any that they have been unable to trace and will insert an acknowledgement in future editions upon notification of the fact.

INDEX